GOSPEL MUSIC

Motivation Through Song

MICHAEL E. PAYTON, MA

authorHOUSE®

AuthorHouse™
1663 Liberty Drive
Bloomington, IN 47403
www.authorhouse.com
Phone: 833-262-8899

Published by AuthorHouse 09/28/2023

ISBN: 979-8-8230-1551-6 (sc)
ISBN: 979-8-8230-1552-3 (e)

Library of Congress Control Number: 2023918586

Print information available on the last page.

This book is printed on acid-free paper.

DEDICATED TO:

Othel and Dorothy Lewis
Followers of Christ
and
Gospel Music

CONTENTS

FOREWORD

It goes without debate that Jesus Christ is the greatest motivator in the history of mankind. The supreme sacrifice given on the cross serves, as nothing else could, the best possible motivation for wanting to live within the beauty and love of Christianity.

As we look through the pages of the Bible, we see so many other motivating situations that have convinced people to dedicate their lives to God and accept His son as their personal Lord and Savior. From the parting of the sea to giving a blind man sight, and so many more, the glorious miracles Jesus Christ performed while on Earth leave no doubt that there is not any other way one would ever want to spend eternity.

Today, the word of God is spread throughout the world not just in Bible readings or sermons by Sunday school preachers but also by the universal language of music.

Music ministry has been a part of many worship services throughout the generations. In different parts of the world the music varies but the message is always the same.

As I researched the songs presented over these pages, I decided it would be more appropriate to discuss a variation of songs from contemporary to traditional. Some of the songs are from Southern Baptist, Apostolic, Pentecostal, Christian rock, Christian country and other selected Christian venues.

Let me say my intention in writing this book was never to be a music critic or give a music review. My only desire was to point out from various parts of each song the motivational impact made on the listener. Each one of the fifty songs discussed, in my opinion, is an excellent Christian song, well written and with beautiful and inspiring music. It is my hope that every reader of this book has the opportunity to eventually listen and enjoy each.

I have tried to give a brief background for each song, credit to the writers and composers, and my opinion on how various verses of the songs motivate people in their worship of God and their acceptance of Jesus Christ as Lord and Savior.

At the end of each song, I have added a small devotional thought and a reflection page for the reader to think about the feelings they experience as they read the song verses and their thoughts on the impact it may make on their worship, or whether it helped strengthen their faith and why.

Finally, I realize that many readers may disagree with my interpretations of some of the verses discussed. It is not important to any reader that they should agree with my interpretations and opinions, but rather that they let the songs impact them in a manner that personally motivates and strengthens their faith.

Please enjoy.

CHAPTER 1

"OUR GOD"

Written by: Chris Tomlin

One of my favorite parts of the Bible is the *Book of Psalms.* "Our God," in my opinion, could have easily been in a verse of *The Book of Psalms.*

"Our God," is a testimony and song of praise for God. The story told is that of a God that is all loving, all powerful and all providing. As many of the psalms are praises of God written generations ago, "Our God," is indeed a well written and well thought out song of praise and gratitude.

"Our God," written by Chris Tomlin, is a highly motivational and contemporary Christian song performed with enthusiasm and emotion. Looking at some of the key verses you can see and feel the motivation to accept Christ in our lives and the desire to want our families, friends and others we love to do the same.

"Water You turned into wine..." the opening phrase itself indicates the miracle power of God.

"Opened the eyes of the blind..." not only alludes to Jesus giving a blind man his sight but also to the many nonbelievers who witnessed His works and accepted Him as Savior.

"Our God is healer, awesome in power... " tells us there is no problem, regardless how big or difficult, that God can't handle.

"Out of the ashes we rise..." implies how we were brought from nothing to sons and daughters through grace.

"God You are higher than any other..." is our acknowledgement that we believe and accept Jesus Christ as our personal Lord and Savior and we refuse to accept any other God.

"And if our God is for us, then who could ever stop us…" as well as "…and if our God is with us then who can stand against…" both say our acceptance of Jesus Christ is our shield against harm from anyone and our ticket to eternal salvation.

"Our God," is a powerful motivational tool for Christians to not only rejoice in their salvation but also very powerful in motivating nonbelievers to be saved.

"Water You turned into wine
Opened the eyes of the blind
There's no one like You"

"None like you
Into the darkness You shine
Out of the ashes we rise
There's no one like You
None like you"

"Our God is greater, Our God is stronger
God You are higher than any other
Our God is Healer, awesome in power
Our God, our God"

"Into the darkness You shine
Out of the ashes we rise
No one like You
None like You"

"Our God is greater, our God is stronger
God You are higher than any other
Our God is healer, awesome in power
Our God, our God"

"Our God is greater, our God is stronger
God You are higher than any other
Our God is healer, awesome in power
Our God, our God"

"And if our God is for us, then who could ever stop us
And if our God is with us, then what can stand against
And if our God is for us, then who could ever stop us
And if our God is with us, that what can stand against
Then what can stand against"

"Our God is greater, our God is stronger
God You are higher than any other
Our God is healer, awesome in power
Our God, our God
Our God is greater, our God is stronger
God you are higher than any other
Our God is healer, awesome in power
Our God, our God"

"And if our God is for us, then who could ever stop us
And if our God is with us, then what can stand against
And if our God is for us, then who can ever stop us
And if our God is with us, then what can stand against
Then what can stand against
Then what can stand against"

*"If you openly declare that Jesus is Lord and believe
in your heart that God raised Him from the dead
you will be saved. For it is by believing in your
heart that you are made right with God, and it is by
openly declaring your faith that you are saved."*
Romans 10:9-10 (NLT)

REFLECTION PAGE

WHAT IS YOUR FIRST REACTION AFTER LISTENING/READING THIS SONG?

DID THIS SONG INSPIRE YOU TO INCREASE YOUR RELATIONSHIP WITH GOD? WHY?

HOW MUCH DOES MUSIC MINISTRY FIT INTO YOUR WORSHIP?

CHAPTER 2

"GOD OF THIS CITY"

Written by: Bluetree, Aaron Boyd, Andrew McCann, Ian Jordan
Peter Comfort, Peter Kernaghan, Richard Bleakley
"God of this City," lyrics @Capital Christian Music Group,
Capitol Publishing, Universal Music Publishing Group

Singer/Songwriter Chris Tomlin is credited by many with writing "God of this City," but in reality *Songfacts* reports it was composed by the Northern Irish group Bluetree who recorded it on their 2007 album "Greater Things."

Tomlin explained the first time he heard the song was when he was in Ireland playing at a worship night concert in Belfast: "There was this band who played before us named Bluetree who played the song. It was their song in their church, that they'd written, and it just caught me. We were doing this tour and I knew I was going to be singing in cities all over the world and it would be amazing so I asked, 'This song has come out of you guys, could I record it and taken it with us for our Passion Tour?' And they were like, 'yeah man, we'd love that.' It's amazing to hear it here in the United States. It's become such a theme song, especially in tough times this song becomes a rallying cry."

The motivational impact of "God of this City," can easily be seen in videos and felt just by listening. It has become very popular in contemporary church music as each verse motivates and inspires service after service.

"You're the God of this City," the very first words in the song, implies that the word "city" refers to the world, mankind in general.

"You're the light in this darkness," reminds us that darkness is the troubles and trials we go through and the knowledge that God is the answer.

"You're the hope to the hopeless," tells us that with God all things really are possible and hope is always available.

"You're the peace to the restless," indicates that peace is eternal salvation through our Lord and Savior Jesus Christ.

"For greater things have yet to come," may very well be the most motivational phrase in the song. This sentence tells us that as good, great and awesome God has been to us, the best is yet to come.

"And greater things are still to be done here," motivates all of us to be followers of Jesus for no matter how well we may think our lives are now they are nothing compared to what will be done with our lives by accepting Him as our personal Lord and Savior.

"You're the God of this city
You're the King of these people
You're the Lord of this nation
You are"

"You're the light in this darkness
You're the hope to the hopeless
You're the peace to the restless
You are"

"There is no one like our God
There is no one like our God"

"For greater things have yet to come
And greater things are still to be done in
this city
Greater things have yet to come
And greater things are still to be done in
this city"

"You're the God of this city
You're the King of these people
You're the Lord of this nation
You are"

"You're the light in this darkness
You're the hope to the hopeless
You're the peace to the restless
You are"

"There is no one like our God
There is no one like our God"

"For greater things have yet to come
And greater things are still to be done in
this city
Greater things have yet to come
And greater things are still to be done in
this city"

"Greater things have yet to come
And greater things are still to be done
here"

"There is no one like our God
There is no one like you, God"

"For greater things have yet to come
And greater things are still to be done in
this city
Greater things have yet to come
And greater things are still to be done"

"We believe, we believe in You God"

"Greater things have yet to come
And greater things are still to be done in
this city
Greater things have yet to come
And greater things are still to be done
here
Greater things, still to be done here
Ooh"

"You must crave pure spiritual
milk so that you will grow into
a full experience of salvation.
Cry out for this nourishment."

1 Peter 2:2 (NLT)

REFLECTION PAGE

WHAT IS YOUR FIRST REACTION AFTER LISTENING/READING THIS SONG?

DID THIS SONG INSPIRE YOU TO INCREASE YOUR RELATIONSHIP WITH GOD? WHY?

HOW MUCH DOES MUSIC MINISTRY FIT INTO YOUR WORSHIP?

CHAPTER 3

"HOW GREAT IS OUR GOD"

Written by: Chris Tomlin, Ed Cash, Jesse Reeves
Lyrics @Capitol Christian Music Group, Capitol
CMG Publishing, Music Services, Inc.

Spiritual songs have been and still are being written honoring God and many give the author's description of Him in the song's message. Most of those songs are not only praiseworthy but emotional. "How Great is Our God" stands out as a popular contemporary praise song played throughout churches across this land.

"The splendor of a King, clothed in majesty...," gives an immediate picture of what many visualize as an image of God, which confirms His reality in the listener's mind.

"Age to age He stands, and time is in His hands, beginning and the end..." illustrates that God always has been and always will be. These words tell us how awesome and powerful God is, to have created our universe's very existence, nourished mankind from the beginning and will continue to guide us throughout eternity.

"The Godhead Three in One, Father, Spirit, Son..." very clearly and directly defines God. No better description is needed.

"You're the name above all names..." tells us that the name of God dominates believer's thoughts and actions while, "You are worthy of our praise..." exemplifies the love, respect and admiration all Christians unconditionally have for God.

"The splendor of a King, clothed in
majesty
Let all the Earth rejoice
All the Earth rejoice"

"He wraps himself in light
And darkness tries to hide
And trembles at His voice
Trembles at His voice"

"How great is our God, sing with me
How great is our God, and all will see
How great, how great is our God"

"Age to age He stands
And time is in His hands
Beginning and the end
Beginning and the end"

"The Godhead Three and One
Father, Spirit, Son
The Lion and the Lamb
The Lion and the Lamb"

"How great is our God, sing with me
How great is our God, and all will see
How great, how great is our God"

"Name above all names (how great is our
God, sing with me)
Worthy of our praise (how great is our
God, and all will see)
My heart will sing
How great is our God"

"You're the name above all names (how
great is our God, sing with me)
You are worthy of our praise (how great
is our God, and all will see)
And my heart will sing
How great is our God"

"How great is our God, sing with me
How great is our God, and all will see
How great, how great, is our God"

"How great is our God, sing with me
How great is our God, and all will see
How great, how great is our God"

"How great is our God, sing with me
How great is our God, and all will see
How great, how great is our God"

*"Cling tightly to your faith in Christ
and always keep your conscience
clear, doing what you know is right."*
1 Timothy 1:19 TLB

REFLECTION PAGE

WHAT IS YOUR FIRST REACTION AFTER LISTENING/READING THIS SONG?

DID THIS SONG INSPIRE YOU TO INCREASE YOUR RELATIONSHIP WITH GOD? WHY?

HOW MUCH DOES MUSIC MINISTRY FIT INTO YOUR WORSHIP?

CHAPTER 4

"I CAN ONLY IMAGINE"

Written by: MercyMe

Reading the Bible and our imaginations are the only two ways we have to comprehend what heaven may look like. "I Can Only Imagine," asks the question all Christians ask daily: What does Heaven look like?

We all have only our separate ideas and thoughts of what Heaven looks like, what will we look like, who will we see, and what will we do?

Questions about Heaven have been asked for generations by both believers and nonbelievers. "I can Only Imagine," immediately takes us back into our early years in Sunday schools where so many questions about God, church, life, death and birth first came into our minds.

"I can only imagine
What it will be like
When I walk by your side
I can only imagine
What my eyes would see
When Your face is before me
I can only imagine
Yeah"

"Surrounded by Your glory
What will my heart feel
Will I dance for You Jesus

Or in awe of You be still
Will I stand in Your presence
Or to my knees will I fall
Will I sing hallelujah
Will I be able to speak at all
I can only imagine"

"I can only imagine
When that day comes
And I find myself
Standing in the Son
I can only imagine
When all I will do
Is forever, forever worship You
I can only imagine, yeah
I can only imagine"

"Surrounded by Your glory
What will my heart feel
Will I dance for You Jesus
Or in awe of You be still
Will I stand in Your presence
Or to my knees will I fall
Will I sing hallelujah
Will I be able to speak at all
I can only imagine, yeah
I can only imagine"

"Will I dance for You, Jesus
Or in awe of You be still
Will I stand in your presence
Or to my knees will I fall
Will I sing hallelujah
Will I be able to speak at all"

"I can only imagine, yeah
I can only imagine
I can only imagine yeah-yeah
I can only imagine
I can only imagine
I can only imagine"

"I can only imagine
When all I will do
Is forever, forever worship you
I can only imagine."

"Everything comes from God alone,
Everything lives by His power, and
everything is for His glory."
Romans 11:36 TLB

REFLECTION PAGE

WHAT IS YOUR FIRST REACTION AFTER LISTENING/READING THIS SONG?

DID THIS SONG INSPIRE YOU TO INCREASE YOUR RELATIONSHIP WITH GOD? WHY?

HOW MUCH DOES MUSIC MINISTRY FIT INTO YOUR WORSHIP?

CHAPTER 5

"BEAUTIFUL ONE"

Written by: Tim Hughes

"Beautiful One," is a song written by Tim Hughes and released as a single from *By the Tree's* 2004 album, *Hold You High.* "Beautiful One," was originally sung by Jeremy Camp, on his 2004 album, *Carried Me.* The song itself is another great contemporary Christian inspirational and motivational testimony to God.

The Bible teaches us the various names of God: Jehovah, Abba, Father, the Alpha and the Omega, There is no doubt as Christianity continues to grow throughout the world, various other names will be used to honor God.

"Beautiful One," is not only an accurate name for God, but also appropriate. In Genesis 22:14 God is referred to as YAHWEH, "The Lord will provide." Most likely the three most common names of God, particularly in the Old Testament, are Yahweh, Adonal, and Elohim.

"Wonderful, so wonderful is Your unfailing love..." confirms the fact that God created us and will always love us unconditionally.

"Your cross had spoken mercy over me..." describes the sacrifice God made by giving His own Son to save those he loves...US!

"No eye has seen, no ear has heard, no heart could fully know..." implies the great sacrifice of giving your only Son for the salvation of mankind and is inconceivable for any of us to ever imagine the pain and suffering of that event.

"Powerful, so powerful, Your glory fills the skies..." shows the magnificence of power and strength God has throughout the universe.

"The beauty of Your Majesty awakes my heart to see..." illustrates the picturesque landscape not just of our planet but mankind.

"You opened my eyes to Your wonders anew; You captured my heart with this love..." is the feeling of being saved, baptized and starting a new life with new priorities and focus on what is truly important.

"Beautiful One my soul must sing, beautiful One I love..." is indicative of not only being saved and living the Christian life yourself but also spreading the Word to the world.

"Wonderful, so wonderful
Is Your unfailing love
Your cross has spoken mercy over me
No eye has seen, no ear has heard
No heart could fully know"

"How glorious, how beautiful You are"

"Beautiful One I love
You're beautiful One I adore
Beautiful One, my soul must sing"

"Powerful, so powerful
Your glory fills the skies
Your mighty works displayed for all to see
The beauty of your majesty
Awakes my heart to see"

"How marvelous, how wonderful You are"

"Beautiful One I love
You're beautiful One I adore
Beautiful One, my soul must sing
Beautiful One I love
You're beautiful One I adore
Beautiful One, my soul must sing"

"You opened my eyes to Your wonders anew
You captured my heart with this love
Cause nothing on earth is as beautiful as You
You opened my eyes to Your wonders anew
You captured my heart with this love
Cause nothing on earth is as beautiful as You"

"Beautiful One I love
You're beautiful One I adore
Beautiful One, my soul must sing
Beautiful One I love
You're beautiful One I adore
Beautiful One, my soul must sing"

"And You opened my eyes to Your wonders anew
You captured my heart with this love
Because nothing on earth is as beautiful as You."

> *"Know thou the God of thy father, and*
> *serve Him with a perfect heart and*
> *with a willing mind; for the Lord*
> *searcheth all hearts, and*
> *understands all the imaginations*
> *of the thoughts."*
> 1 Chronicles 28:9 KJV

REFLECTION PAGE

WHAT IS YOUR FIRST REACTION AFTER LISTENING/READING THIS SONG?

DID THIS SONG INSPIRE YOU TO INCREASE YOUR RELATIONSHIP WITH GOD? WHY?

HOW MUCH DOES MUSIC MINISTRY FIT INTO YOUR WORSHIP?

CHAPTER 6

"AMAZING GRACE"

Words by: John Newton
From: Carroll & Clayton's Virginia Harmony
Arranged by: Edwin O. Excell

If you ask anyone to name a Christian song most likely the first, they will mention is "Amazing Grace." Possibly the best known of all religious songs in our lifetime "Amazing Grace" indeed graces the sanctuaries of churches throughout our land every Sunday morning.

Initially a Christian hymn, "Amazing Grace," first published in 1779 with the words written by John Newton (1725-1807), an English Anglican clergyman, later became one of the most popular Christian songs in the United States.

Newton had a controversial and colorful life prior to writing the Christian classic. A member of the Royal Navy and after leaving its service, becoming involved with the Atlantic slave trade where in 1748 after surviving a violent storm destroying his ship off the coast of County Donegal, Ireland, he cried out for God to have mercy, the event which started his spiritual conversion. After surviving the storm Newton eventually ended his slave trading and seafaring in 1755 and began studying Christian theology.

In 1764 Newton was ordained in the Church of England where he began to write hymns. "Amazing Grace," was written to reflect a sermon on New Year's Day of 1773. There is no record as to whether music was originally written with the words. In 1835, according to Wikipedia,

American composer William Walker wrote the tune which is the version most used today.

"Amazing Grace," expresses the message that forgiveness and redemption are possible regardless of our sins through the grace of God and our inclusion in the Kingdom of Heaven will be assured if we accept Jesus Christ in our hearts and souls as our personal Lord and Savior.

"Amazing Grace how sweet the sound that saved a wretch like me,..." gives the best motivation anyone could want: grace by God is available to all and is free for the asking. No matter what you may have done, how bad you may think you were, no matter how rich or poor, healthy or sick you may be, the grace given by God will give you eternal salvation in heaven.

"I once was lost but now am found, was blind, but now I see..." lets us know that our past can and will be forgiven through the grace of God and that although we may have lived a life of sin it will all vanish by just asking God for forgiveness.

"Twas grace that taught my heart to fear and grace my fears relieved..." describes how once the grace of God comes into your life all fears and sins are washed away and you will have a new life eternal. Now that's motivation!

"Amazing Grace," was indeed an ideal name for this song. Grace by God provided by Jesus Christ paying the ultimate price with His life is a reflection of the love provided by God. It is a love that is so strong for each of us that it is reflected by Him letting His son die for us.

There are many of us who will truthfully say we would die for our children, and I believe there is no doubt we would, but the difference is, how many of us would be willing to die for the sins of other people? It is a fascinating question to ponder. God's grace is truly Amazing!

"Amazing Grace! How sweet the sound, that saved a wretch like me"
"I once was lost, but now am found, was blind but now I see"

"Twas grace that taught my heart to fear, and grace my fears relieved,
How precious did that grace appear the hour I first believed"

"Through many dangers, toils and snares, I have already come, tis grace hath brought me safe thus far and grace will lead me home"

"The Lord has promised good to me, His word my hope secures, He will my shield
and portion be as long as life endures. And when this flesh and heart shall fail and mortal
life shall cease, I shall possess within the veil, a life of joy and peace."

"When we've been there ten thousand years, bright shining as the sun, we've no less days to sing God's praise than when we first begun."

*"They that wait upon the Lord shall
renew their strength. They shall mount
up with wings like eagles, they shall run
and not be weary, they shall walk and
not faint."*

Isaiah 40:31 TLB

REFLECTION PAGE

WHAT IS YOUR FIRST REACTION AFTER LISTENING/READING THIS SONG?

DID THIS SONG INSPIRE YOU TO INCREASE YOUR RELATIONSHIP WITH GOD? WHY?

HOW MUCH DOES MUSIC MINISTRY FIT INTO YOUR WORSHIP?

CHAPTER 7

"Because He Lives"

Words by: William J. and Gloria Gaither
Music by: William J. Gaither

As reported in *"Singing News,"* "Because He Lives," has recently celebrated its 50th anniversary and is now one of the most popular songs written by William and Gloria Gaither.

Gloria, in an interview with *"Singing News,"* stated, "We live our lives with confidence because the Resurrection is true. Life wins! And because our Lord is alive, we can trust Him with our future, so honestly we wrote this song for us."

When talking with *"Oasis Church,"* Gloria revealed she wrote the lyrics in the late 1960s when she was pregnant with her and William's third child and the couple was adjusting to an additional member of their family and "God graced us with an unexpected gentle, calming peace."

Gloria recalled the experience as if God granted her a calmness and assurance that only He could impart. She went on to say that "we all have times of anxiety and anguish and more importantly we also have hope and a certain future because we too are in God's hands."

A GRAMMY nomination of the song marked the 50th anniversary and was the focus of a TBN special *"Because He Lives: An Easter Celebration,"* presented by the Gospel Music Association.

"Because He Lives," transcends generations and motivates all ages listening at any given time. Many different artists including Alabama, Matt Maher, Bradley Walker, Kristin Chenoweth, Carrie Underwood, and

Harry Connick Jr., have all recorded various renditions as the popularity of the song only continues to grow.

When we look at the song and what appears to be its deeper meaning which motivates someone toward Christianity, we look at the first few sentences. "God sent His son, they called Him Jesus, He came to heal, love and forgive," gives us three reasons Jesus came to the earth. Hence, Jesus came to Earth so that God could open a door into Heaven for anyone that wanted to come; that's the bottom line to Jesus coming to earth. He was sent by God to prepare us for our place in Heaven. God wants us there and he has provided the way, we just have to follow the course He has planned.

"He lived and died to buy our pardon," is a motivation of love. It would be difficult to say that there is anything greater in love than for another giving his/her only child to die for you, not to mention your sins as well.

The stanza, "How sweet it is to hold a newborn baby and feel the pride and joy He gives; but greater still the calmer assurance this child can face uncertain days because He lives," highlights the song's entire theme because it pointedly says that because of the life, death and resurrection of our Lord Jesus Christ that we all will be assured the opportunity to spend eternity in Heaven.

The chorus, "Because He lives, I can face tomorrow, because He lives, I know all fear is gone, because I know He holds the future, and life is worth living just because He lives," reinforces and motivates belief to exactly why God sent Jesus to us and what the purpose of Jesus being sent here was for: Because God loves all of us!

"God sent His only son, they called Him Jesus
He came to love, heal and forgive
He lived and died to buy my pardon
An empty grave is there to prove my Savior lives"

"Because He lives I can face tomorrow
Because He lives all fear is gone
Because I know He holds the future
And life is worth living
Just because He lives"

"How sweet to hold a newborn baby
And feel the pride and joy he gives
But greater still the calm assurance
This child can face uncertain days
Because He lives"

"Because He lives I can face tomorrow
Because He lives all fear is gone
Because I know He holds the future
And life is worth the living
Just because He lives"

"And then one day I'll cross that river
I'll fight life's final war and pain
and then as death gives way to victory
I'll see the lights of glory and I'll know He reigns"

"Because He lives I can face tomorrow
Because He lives all fear is gone
Because I know He holds the future
and life is worth living
Just because He lives."

> *"But God commendeth His love toward
> us, in that, while we were yet sinners,
> Christ died for us."*
>
> Romans 5:8 KIV

REFLECTION PAGE

WHAT IS YOUR FIRST REACTION AFTER LISTENING/READING THIS SONG?

DID THIS SONG INSPIRE YOU TO INCREASE YOUR RELATIONSHIP WITH GOD? WHY?

HOW MUCH DOES MUSIC MINISTRY FIT INTO YOUR WORSHIP?

CHAPTER 8

"How Great Thou Art"

WORDS & MUSIC: STUART K. HINE

Most likely no other Christian hymn has inspired and motivated Christians and non-Christians across the world more than "How Great Thou Art."

According to Wikipedia, "How Great Thou Art," is a Christian hymn based on an original Swedish hymn, "O Store Gud," written in 1885 by Carl Boberg (1859-1940). The English version of the song along with its title change occurred in 1949 by English missionary Stuart K. Hine.

The original inspiration for the song is believed to be when Boberg was walking home from church in Kronoback, Sweden, and was listening to church bells. Suddenly a storm got Boberg's attention and then just as suddenly as it made its appearance it changed to a peaceful calm which Boberg observed over Monsteras Bay. Boberg then eventually created the song based on his thoughts about how great it was that something so powerful and strong could leave such a peaceful and beautiful result.

In later years generations of people would be motivated, inspired and in the case of non-believers, directed toward Christianity by the moving words and music of this beautiful song.

As the song spread throughout the world over the generations many different ministers, choirs and revivals knew "How Great Thou Art," was a necessity for any serious event. Over the years, such artists as George Beverly Shea, Cliff Borrows and Carrie Underwood have inspired many with their renditions and the Billy Graham Crusades often had choirs singing the hymn loud and clear.

"How Great Thou Art," was ranked second (after "Amazing Grace") on a list of favorite hymns of all time in a survey by *Christianity Today* magazine in 2001. The song was also voted the British public's favorite hymn by BBC's *Songs of Praise*.

As we look at the song, the words, "O Lord my God when I in awesome wonder, consider all the worlds Thy hands have made," immediately you feel the extreme endless power of God. That verse alone tells us He is the creator of all things.

"I see the stars, I hear the rolling thunder, the power throughout the universe displayed..." is a definite picture of power, strength and knowledge telling all of us who the true "I Am" really is.

"Then sings my soul, my Savior God to Thee, how great Thou art, how great Thou art," is the sounds of a new born Christian finding God and the great mysteries and wonders of heaven and the hereafter spent with our Lord and Savior Jesus Christ.

"O Lord my God, when I in awesome wonder,
Consider all the worlds Thy hands have made,
I see the stars, I hear the rolling thunder,
Thy power throughout the universe displayed"

"Then sing my soul, my Savior God to Thee
How great Thou art,
How great Thou art"

"Then sing my soul, my Savior God to Thee
How great Thou art,
How great Thou art"

"And when I think that God, His Son not sparing
Sent Him to die, I scarce can take it in
That on the cross, my burden gladly bearing
He bled and died to take away my sin"

"Then sings my soul, my Savior God to Thee
How great Thou art, how great Thou art"

"Then sings my soul, my Savior God to Thee
How great Thou art, how great Thou art"

"When Christ shall come, with soul of acclamation
and take me home, what joy shall fill my heart
Then I shall bow in humble adoration
And then proclaim, my God how great Thou art"

"Then sings my soul, my Savior God to Thee
How great Thou art, how great Thou art
Then sings my soul, my Savior God to Thee
How great Thou art
How great Thou art"

*"Everyone who hears these words of
mine and puts them into practice is
like a wise man who built his house
on the rock."*

Matthew 7:24 NIV

REFLECTION PAGE

WHAT IS YOUR FIRST REACTION AFTER LISTENING/READING THIS SONG?

DID THIS SONG INSPIRE YOU TO INCREASE YOUR RELATIONSHIP WITH GOD? WHY?

HOW MUCH DOES MUSIC MINISTRY FIT INTO YOUR WORSHIP?

CHAPTER 9

"HE'S GOT THE WHOLE WORLD IN HIS HANDS"

Original Author: Unknown

"He's Got the Whole World in His Hands," is one of the most well-known and long-lasting Christian hymns ever written, which is ironic as there has been no definitive author ever identified although there have been many different renditions by many different writers and singers over the years.

God Tube reports that the song arose out of the oral tradition of African Americans and has become one of the most widely known and loved hymns ever sung by young and old throughout the world. Like other songs coming from an oral tradition, it has many variations in both text and tune.

The song is particularly popular with Sunday schools and churches which teach God's position as the creator and ruler of the world. The text confesses the same theme of the Lord's cosmic rule that is proclaimed in the kingship psalms such as Psalm 47 and Psalm 93-99: "The Lord reigns!" The stanzas give examples of aspects of the "whole world" - nature, human creatures, everything and everyone.

"He's got the whole world in His hands, He's got the whole world in His hands, He's got the whole world in His hands..." motivates us toward admiration and respect for the awesome power God has and that He alone is totally and completely responsible for the creation and existence of everything that happens on this planet.

"He's got you and me brother in His hands, He's got you and me brother in His hands, He's got you and me brother in His hands...." tells us all men and their actions are under His supreme control and judgment, both biological brothers and brothers in Christ.

"He's got you and me sister in His hands, He's got you and me sister in His hands, He's got you and me sister in His hands...." tells us that as He does with men He also has total control and judgment of biological sisters and sisters in Christ.

"He's got the whole world in His hands," motivates all of us to understand that when we say God has the entire world in His hands, it impresses upon us God's supreme power, love and care for all mankind. We understand that God truly holds the creation of people, animals. the elements of weather (sun, rain, snow, sleet, hail), the land, sea, air and their destinies in His hands.

"He's got the whole world in His hands
He's got the whole world in His hands
He's got the whole world in His hands
He's got the whole world in His hands"

"He's got the wind and the rain in His hands
He's got the wind and the rain in His hands
He's got the wind and the rain in His hands
He's got the whole world in His hands."

"He's got the little bitty baby in His hands
He's got the little bitty baby in His hands
He's got the little bitty baby in His hands
He's got the whole world in His hands"

"He's got you and me sister in His hands
He's got you and me sister in His hands
He's got you and me sister in His hands
He's got the whole world in His hands"

"He's got you and me brother in His hands
He's got you and me brother in His hands
He's got you and me brother in His hands
He's got the whole world in His hands"

"He's got everybody in His hands
He's got everybody in His hands
He's got everybody in His hands
He's got the whole world in His hands."

> *"His divine power has given us*
> *everything we need for life and*
> *godliness through our knowledge of*
> *him who called us by his own glory*
> *and goodness."*
>
> 2 Peter 1:3 NIV

REFLECTION PAGE

WHAT IS YOUR FIRST REACTION AFTER LISTENING/READING THIS SONG?

DID THIS SONG INSPIRE YOU TO INCREASE YOUR RELATIONSHIP WITH GOD? WHY?

HOW MUCH DOES MUSIC MINISTRY FIT INTO YOUR WORSHIP?

CHAPTER 10

PEACE IN THE VALLEY

Words and Music by: Thomas A. Dorsey

"Peace in the Valley," was written in 1937 by Thomas A. Dorsey, as reported by "The Scottspot" website. Dorsey was a member of the Pilgrim Baptist Church in Chicago, Illinois and had began to play a major role in directing music of the church.

Including "Peace in the Valley," Dorsey would eventually write hundreds of gospel songs known throughout the world.

Thomas would become the best known African American composer of gospel music in America. His hymns became favorites in churches both in the North and South regions of the United States.

Thomas wrote "Peace in the Vally" shortly before Hitler sent his military into Western Europe. According to "The Scottspot," Thomas was on a train going through southern Indiana on his way to Cincinnati when he passed through a valley on the train. Horses, cows, and sheep were all grazing together in the valley regions, with a little brook running through. Everything seemed so peaceful it caused him to wonder what was wrong with mankind.

As he traveled, he wrote the words and the tune he set would be a mix of gospel, blues and country. Later, country singers would pick up on the song and eventually it became one of the ten best-known country songs of all time.

Before his death, President Lyndon B. Johnson requested that the hymn be sung at his funeral. Anitia Bryant was chosen to honor that request.

"I'm tired and I'm weary, but I must toil on, till the Lord comes to call me away..." tells of the obligation Christians have to the Lord Jesus Christ to continue working spreading His word regardless of how physical or emotionally demanding it may be.

"Where the morning is bright and the Lamb is the light, and the night is fair as the day...." implies the journey will be long but the way will be safe for the Lord will lead the way.

"There will be peace in the valley for me some day, there will be peace in the valley for me...." says the day will come after the journey is complete when we can rest peacefully in the valley of Heaven for eternity.

"I pray no more sorrow and sadness or trouble will be, there will be peace in the valley for me..." lets us know once we have arrived in Heaven and the place prepared for us by Jesus, there will no longer be any worry of sickness, regret, or sin, just a beautiful and eternal rest, happiness and love.

"There the flowers will be blooming, the grass will be green, and the skies will be clear and serene, the sun ever shines, giving one endless beam and clouds there will ever be seen......" describes the beauty and brilliance of our eternal home.

"I'm tired and I'm weary, but I must toil on
till the Lord come to call me away;
where the morning is bright and the Lamb is the light
and the night is fair as the day."

There will be peace in the valley for me some day,
there will be peace in the valley for me.
I pray no more sorrow and sadness or trouble will be
there will be peace in the valley for me."

"There the flowers will be blooming, the grass will be green,
and the skies will be clear and serene;
the sun ever shines, giving one endless beam
and the clouds there will ever be seen."

"There will be peace in the valley for me some day,
there will be peace in the valley for me.
I pray no more sorrow and sadness or trouble will be
there will be peace in the valley for me."

"There the bear will be gentle, the wolf will be tame,
and the lion will lay down with the lamb;
the host from the wild will be led by a Child and
I'll be changed from the creature I am."

"There will be peace in the valley for me some day,
there will be peace in the valley for me.
I pray no more sorrow and sadness or trouble will be
there will be peace in the valley for me."

> *"Come to me and I will give you rest-all of you who
> work so hard beneath a heavy yoke."*
> Matthew 11:28 TLB

REFLECTION PAGE

WHAT IS YOUR FIRST REACTION AFTER LISTENING/READING THIS SONG?

DID THIS SONG INSPIRE YOU TO INCREASE YOUR RELATIONSHIP WITH GOD? WHY?

HOW MUCH DOES MUSIC MINISTRY FIT INTO YOUR WORSHIP?

CHAPTER 11

"House of the Lord"

Written by: Phil Wickham and Jonathan Smith

"House of the Lord," was released April 2, 2021, by Phil Wickham, a contemporary Christian musician and was the second single from his eighth album, *Hymn of Heaven*. The song itself was written by both Wickham and Jonathan Smith who produced the single.

"House of the Lord," rose to number one on the US *Hot Christian Songs* chart. The song also went to number twelve on the *Bubbling Under Hot 100* chart. At the 2022 *GMA Dove Awards* "House of the Lord" received two nominations for Song of the Year and Pop/Contemporary Recorded Song of the Year.

Wikipedia reported that Jonathan Andre of *365 Days of Inspiring Media* gave a very positive review saying it "keeps our focus on things above, to realign from our own immediate circumstances, to being reminded that God is in our midst wherever we are, that His moving into our lives, either through healing physically, mentally, or even spiritually, needs to be declared and recognized, and such a song as this, does this very fact."

Since its release and recognition on the various Christian radio stations and magazines, "House of the Lord" has become a regular at many contemporary and traditional Sunday church services and revivals throughout the country.

"We worship the God who was, we worship the God who is, We worship the God who evermore will be....." is the true definition of God: Always was, Always is, and Always will be.

"He opened the prison doors, He parted the raging sea, My God, He holds the Victory..." is the true and ultimate definition of God's awesome and ever-present power.

"There is joy in the house of the Lord, there's joy in the house of the Lord today...." is reflective of the celebration of salvation granted to all of us who believe.

"We sing to the God who heals, we sing to the God who saves, we sing to the God who always makes a way, cause He hung up on that cross, then He rose up from that grave, My God's still rolling stones away..." describes the enthusiastic and joyful praising all Christians have for His love and caring for all His children and His continuous protection of all His children.

"We were the beggars, now we're royalty, we were the prisoners, now we're running free, we are forgiven, accepted, redeemed by His grace, let the house of the Lord sing praise....." describes how beautiful and rewarding it is for accepting Jesus Christ as our personal Lord and Savior.

"There's joy in the house of the Lord, there's joy in the house of the Lord today, and we won't be quiet, we shout out Your praise (we gonna shout out Your praise)" is a very vocal and exciting thankfulness for our precious Lord and Savior Jesus Christ.

"We worship the God who was
We worship the God who is
We worship the God who evermore will be
He opened the prison doors
He parted the raging sea
My God, He holds the victory"

"There's joy in the house of the Lord
There's joy in the house of the Lord
today
And we won't be quiet
We shout out Your praise"

"There's joy in the house of the Lord
Our God is surely in this place
And we won't be quiet

We shout out Your praise
(Oh-oh, oh) we shout out Your praise
(Oh-oh, oh)"

"We sing to the God who heals
We sing to the God who saves
We sing to the God who always makes a way
'Cause He hung up on that cross
Then He rose up from that grave
My God's still rolling stones away"

"There's joy in the house of the Lord
There's joy in the house of the Lord
today
And we won't be quiet
We shout out Your praise"

"There's joy in the house of the Lord
Our God is surely in this place
And we won't be quiet
We shout out Your praise"

"Cause we were the beggars
Now we're royalty
We were the prisoners
Now we're running free
We are forgiven, accepted
Redeemed by His grace
Let the house of the Lord sing praise"

"There's joy in the house of the Lord
(there is joy in the house)
There's joy in the house of the Lord
today
And we won't be quiet (oh yeah)
We shout out Your praise (I wanna shout
out Your praise)"

"There's joy in the house of the Lord
(there is joy)
Our God is surely in this place (there is
joy)
And we won't be quiet
We shout out Your praise (we gonna
shout out Your praise)"

"There's joy in the house of the Lord
There's joy in the house of the Lord
today
And we won't be quiet
We shout out Your praise (we gonna
shout out Your praise)"

"There's joy in the house of the Lord
(there is joy, there is joy)
Our God is surely in this place (joy in this
place)
And we won't be quiet (we won't be
quiet)
We shout out Your praise"

"We shout out Your praise
There is joy in the house, there is joy in
the house today
We shout out Your praise
We shout out Your praise"

*"Now that you have been set free from
sin and have become slaves to God,
the benefit you reap leads to holiness,
and the result is eternal life. For the
wages of sin is death, but the gift of
God is eternal life in Christ Jesus our Lord.*
Romans 6:22-23 NIV

REFLECTION PAGE

WHAT IS YOUR FIRST REACTION AFTER LISTENING/READING THIS SONG?

DID THIS SONG INSPIRE YOU TO INCREASE YOUR RELATIONSHIP WITH GOD? WHY?

HOW MUCH DOES MUSIC MINISTRY FIT INTO YOUR WORSHIP?

CHAPTER 12

"HOLY WATER"

Written by: Ed Cash, Scott Cash, Franni Cash,
Martin Cash, Andrew Bergthold
Producer: We the Kingdom

We the Kingdom's debut entry on the US *Hot Christian Songs* chart having peaked at number 2 was "Holy Water." The song, also the highest-charting song of their career, peaked at number 6 on *Billboard's Bubbling Under Hot 100* chart. "Holy Water," was nominated for the *GMA Dove Awards,* for the Song of the Year and Pop/Contemporary Recorded Song of the Year and *"Holy Water"* earned a Grammy Award nomination for Best Contemporary Christian Music Performance/Song at the 2021 Grammy Awards.

"Holy Water," was released by We the Kingdom, September 13, 2019 as the second single from *Live at the Wheelhouse* (2019). Wikipedia reports an acoustic version of the song by the band was released on the *Live Acoustic Sessions* EP in March 2020.

As one of Christian music's most popular contemporary songs, "Holy Water" is motivational, emotional, and powerful. The song title is reference to the spiritual presence of God in our lives and His feeding us of His Holy Word. The song leads us to inspirational highs and praises God for all His wonderful blessings.

"God I'm on my knees again, God I'm begging please again, I need you, Oh I need you...." refers to the realization of the supreme importance of God in our lives and uninhibited humbleness with which we come to Him for our every need.

"Your forgiveness, is like sweet, sweet honey on my lips, like the sound of a symphony to my ears, like Holy water on my skin..." defines the point that forgiveness is the ultimate gift given us by God through Jesus Christ.

"Dead man walking, slave to sin, I wanna know about being born again, I need you, Oh God I need you...." is asking God to teach us how to live life in the light after only existing as a non-believer in the dark.

"I don't wanna abuse your grace, God I need it every day, it's the only thing that ever really makes me wanna change...." is our promise never to take advantage of the greatest gift we will ever receive.

"God, I'm on my knees again
God, I'm begging please again
I need you
Oh, I need you"

"Walking down these desert roads
Water for my thirsty soul
I need you
Oh, I need you"

"Your forgiveness
Is like sweet, sweet honey on my lips
Like the sound of a symphony to my
ears
Like Holy water on my skin"

"Dead man walking, slave to sin
I wanna know about being born again
I need you
Oh, God, I need you"

"So take me to the riverside
Take me under, baptize
I need you
Oh, God I need you"

"Your forgiveness
Is like sweet, sweet honey on my lips
Like the sound of a symphony to my
ears
Like Holy water on my skin
(0n my Skin)"

"I don't wanna abuse your grace
God, I need it every day
It's the only thing that ever really makes
me wanna change"

"I don't wanna abuse your grace
God, I need it every day
It's the only thing that ever really makes
me wanna change"

"Your forgiveness
Is like sweet, sweet honey on my lips
(yes it is)
Like the sound of a symphony to my
ears
It's like Holy water"

"Your forgiveness
Is like sweet, sweet honey on my lips
Like the sound of a symphony on my
ears
It's like Holy water on my skin
It's like Holy water on my skin
It's like Holy water"

*"Listen, my son, accept what I say, and
the years of your life will be many. I
guide you in the way of wisdom and
lead you along straight paths."*
Proverbs 4:10-11 NIV

REFLECTION PAGE

WHAT IS YOUR FIRST REACTION AFTER LISTENING/READING THIS SONG?

DID THIS SONG INSPIRE YOU TO INCREASE YOUR RELATIONSHIP WITH GOD? WHY?

HOW MUCH DOES MUSIC MINISTRY FIT INTO YOUR WORSHIP?

"FROM THE INSIDE OUT"

Written by: Joel Houston (Hillsong)

The Christian Music Minister in an interview with Joel Houston about "From the Inside Out," describing how the song developed and what the song's purpose is, gave an in-depth view of why he wrote the song and why he feels it is one of the most difficult he has ever written.

Houston stated, "That song is probably the hardest song I have ever had to write. It's possible that's because more than any other song I've written it is the essence of me really gaining a revelation of who Christ is and what it means to be a follower. I feel like when I look at the lyrics of that song, it's me unpacking everything I knew to be true about God at that period of my life."

Houston also explained the song developed because it's "the story of a fuller understanding of worship" for himself and "I was maturing as a human being but was also growing in my understanding of faith and my understanding of God....I was really setting myself up to come to terms with how I was going to live my life."

"From the Inside Out," is a very popular, powerful and motivational song with a strong poetic format and is able to increase the intensity of worship with a well-illustrated understanding of grace and mercy.

As pointed out very clearly in *The Christian Music Minister,* the song is really about the Church. As we each individually get the revelation for ourselves to live our lives from the inside out, that translates to a Church that is not inward focused, but one that is outward focused.

"A thousand times I've failed, still Your mercy remains, and should I stumble again I'm caught in Your grace..." illustrates how much God not only loves us but how much He unconditionally loves us regardless of the mistakes we make throughout our lives, we know He will always be there.

"Everlasting, Your light will shine when all else fades, never ending, Your glory goes beyond all fame....." reminds us that no matter what other options we may believe we have to solve our problems there is only one option that will always be there for us and that is His love and caring.

"In my heart and my soul Lord I give you control, consume me from the inside out Lord, let justice and praise become my embrace, to love you from the inside out..." signifies the acceptance of Jesus Christ as our personal Lord and Savior, turning your entire life, physical, emotional and spiritual, to following His word forever.

"And the cry of my heart is to bring You praise, from the inside out, Lord my soul cries out..." illustrates that giving God praises is not just superficial to impress others or make yourself feel good but instead it is a ever-lasting, intense, burning desire constantly in our hearts.

"A thousand times I've failed
Still Your mercy remains
And should I stumble again
I'm caught in Your grace"

"Everlasting
Your light will shine when all else fades
Never ending
Your glory goes beyond all fame"

"Your will above all else
My purpose remains
The art of losing myself
In bringing you grace"

"Everlasting
Your light will shine when all else fades
Never ending
Your glory goes beyond all fame"

"In my heart and my soul
Lord I give you control
Consume me from the inside out,
Lord, let justice and praise
Become my embrace
To love you from the inside out"

"Your will above all else
My purpose remains
The art of losing myself
In bringing You praise"

"Everlasting
Your light will shine when all else fades
Never ending
Your glory goes beyond all fame"

"And the cry of my heart
is to bring You praise
From the inside out
Lord my soul cries out"

"In my heart and my soul
Lord I give you control
Consume me from the inside out,
Lord, let justice and praise
Become my embrace
To love you from the inside out"

"Everlasting
Your light will shine when all else fades
Never ending
Your glory goes beyond all fame"

"And the cry of my heart
is to bring You praise
From the inside out
Lord my soul cries out"

"Everlasting
Your light will shine when all else fades
Never ending
Your glory goes beyond all fame"

"And the cry of my heart
is to bring You praise
From the inside out
Lord my soul cries out"

"From the inside out
Lord my soul cries out."

> *"You will keep in perfect peace him whose mind is steadfast, because he trusts in you. Trust in the LORD forever, for the LORD, the LORD, is the Rock eternal."*
>
> Isaiah 26:3 NIV

REFLECTION PAGE

WHAT IS YOUR FIRST REACTION AFTER LISTENING/READING THIS SONG?

DID THIS SONG INSPIRE YOU TO INCREASE YOUR RELATIONSHIP WITH GOD? WHY?

HOW MUCH DOES MUSIC MINISTRY FIT INTO YOUR WORSHIP?

CHAPTER 14

"FRIEND OF GOD"

Written by: Israel Houghton

The song, "Friend of God," is a lot more meaningful than its lyrics might imply on the surface. As we all know, finding a true friendship is indeed a blessing. When you find someone who is willing to share the good times and the bad it is rare and unique. It is important to realize that when we become believers in the Lord Jesus Christ, God Himself has invested in a permanent relationship with us.

It is important to remember regarding those of us that accept Christianity is our faith in Jesus Christ is present because God gave it to us. A relationship with God exists because of belief, not by our good works, our own efforts or decisions. The only way a relationship with God exists is by grace through faith.

In an article by *Drew Hunter* in July 2018, it is pointed out that there is a big difference between being a servant and a friend. In *John 15:15* Jesus states in part, "No longer do I call you servants, but I have called you friends." A servant only comes when there's something to do, but a friend is welcome anytime. A servant is told what to do, but a friend is told why. A servant will bring the food to the table, but the friend will eat it with you.

Israel Houghton, the writer of "Friend of God," received nominations for song of the year at the 2005 *Dove Awards*. Houghton also has won six *Grammy Awards,* three for Pop/Contemporary Gospel Album and one for Best Traditional Gospel Album.

"I am a friend of God, I am a friend of God, I am a friend of God and He calls me friend...." signifies a confident and secure relationship with God which shows a understanding that God always is thinking of and ready to help us just for asking and believing.

"Who am I that You are mindful of me, that You hear me when I call, is it true that You are thinking of me, how You love me, it's amazing, it's amazing...." implies the remarkable truth we comprehend that the Father of the universe with all He controls can amazingly enough have time to always love and care for us.

"God almighty, Lord of glory, You have called me friend..." reflects the gratitude and love we have for God not only being our heavenly Father and Provider but our true friend.

"I am a friend of God
I am a friend of God
I am a friend of God He calls me friend
Who am I that you are mindful of me
That You hear me when I call
Is it true that You are thinking of me
How You love me it's amazing"

"I am a friend of God
I am a friend of God
I am a friend of God
He calls me friend"

"I am a friend of God
I am a friend of God
I am a friend of God
He calls me friend
Who am I that You are mindful of me
That You hear me when I call
Is it true that You are thinking of me
How You love me
It's amazing, it's amazing, it's amazing"

"I am a friend of God
I am a friend of God
I am a friend of God
He calls me friend"

"God almighty
Lord of glory
You have called me friend"

"God almighty
Lord of glory
You have called me friend"

"I am a friend of God
I am a friend of God
I am a friend of God
He calls me friend"

"I am a friend of God
I am a friend of God
I am a friend of God
He calls me friend"

"He calls me friend
He calls me friend
He calls me friend"

*"You are My friends if you do whatever
I command you. No longer do I call you
servants, for a servant does not know
what his master is doing; but I have called
you friends, for all things that I heard from
My Father I have made known to you."*

John 15: 14-15

REFLECTION PAGE

WHAT IS YOUR FIRST REACTION AFTER LISTENING/READING THIS SONG?

DID THIS SONG INSPIRE YOU TO INCREASE YOUR RELATIONSHIP WITH GOD? WHY?

HOW MUCH DOES MUSIC MINISTRY FIT INTO YOUR WORSHIP?

CHAPTER 15

"SUNDAY SERMONS"

Written by: Anne Wilson, Ben Glover, Jeff Sojka

As much as I love the old-fashioned, traditional Christian hymns I am also a fan of much of the new contemporary Christian music that has continued to grow in popularity and more importantly draw more and more younger people to know our Lord and Savior Jesus Christ.

Music is a great ministry. Music reaches people across the world that may not even speak our language but are moved by the inspiring music and feeling of belonging it gives them.

"Sunday Sermons," is a relatively new contemporary Christian song, written by Anne Wilson with Ben Glover and Jeff Sojka. First released on January 14, 2022, the song was the second single from her album *My Jesus.*

As reported in *Wikipedia,* Wilson in a interview stated in part, "This is my story of growing up in the church since I was a little girl. God used every Sunday sermon to develop a firm foundation in Him. I didn't realize just how deep my roots were in Him from all those years of showing up to church each Sunday morning until I encountered hardships in my life. No matter what happens in life, even losing a loved one, I can always go back to the foundation of truth that the Lord planted in me through each of those sermons. This song is to remind you to cling to the One who's consistent and faithful. Jesus loves you more than you can ever imagine."

"Seven years old, third row pew, John 3:16, something changed in me, red letters coming off the page, flooding my heart with amazing grace, I knew then I believed, and those roots run deep...." is the realization that God has always been a real part of our lives and family has a strong Christian foundation from an early age. There is an understanding that God's Word is powerful and His presence is evident throughout the Bible.

"Oh, I been through some faith shaking hard times yeah, but nothing's gonna make me forget...." shows the knowledge that although it isn't always easy God's word will always protect me.

"Every one of those Sunday sermons, every time that choir would sing, I could hear my Savior calling, telling me how much He loves me, no matter what the world throws at me, I know His word is true, it all started with heart stirring, spirit moving Sunday Sermons.,," reflects the power and meaning of the sermon. The understanding that it is not the preacher just speaking words, it is God speaking the Word through the preacher.

"Devil gon' try and take me out of that church, but you can't take the church out of me, Devil gon' try and take me out of that church, but you can't take the church out of me....." implies that "church" isn't just that building or only one Sunday but church is an intense part of our lives twenty-four hours a day, sleeping and awake, based on faith, love and belief in Jesus Christ.

"Gonna have my worries, well that's part of life, but then I think of those stories 'bout what my God can do, He's still moving like He did back then, born again people, can I get an amen (Amen), we've all seen the proof, He makes all things new...." says life is always going to have problems and worries but faith in our Lord and Savior Jesus Christ will always be our weapon and God our protector.

"Jesus loves me, this I know (this I know), for the Bible tells me so, Jesus loves me, ain't no doubt (ain't no doubt), so I'm gonna keep on talking about, oh yeah...." is testimony that the Lord Jesus Christ does truly love us and our blessings are the only proof we need."

"Seven years old, third row pew
John 3:16, something changed in me
Red letters coming off the page
Flooding my heart with amazing grace
I knew then I believed
And those roots run deep"

"Oh, I been through some faith shaking hard times, yeah
But nothing's gonna make me forget"

"Every one of those Sunday sermons
Every time that choir would sing
I could hear my Savior calling, telling me how much He loves me
No matter what the world throws at me
I know His word is true
It all started with heart stirring, spirit moving Sunday sermons"

"Devil gon' try and take me out of that church
But you can't take the church out of me
Devil gon' try and take me out of that church
But you can't take the church out of me"

"Gonna have my worries, well that's part of life
But then I think of those stories 'bout what my God can do
He's still moving like He did back then
Born again people, can I get an amen? (Amen)
We've all seen the proof
He makes all things new"

"Even all those faith shaking hard times, yeah
I never wanna stop remembering"

"Every one of those Sunday sermons
Every time that choir would sing
I could hear my Savior calling, telling me how much He loves me
No matter what the world throws at me
I know His word is true
It all started with a heart stirring, spirit moving Sunday Sermon"

"Devil gon' try and take me out of that church
But you can't take the church out of me
Devil gon' try and take me out of that church
But you can't take the church out of me"

"Oh-whoa, those Sunday sermons"

"Jesus loves me
This I know (this I know)
For the Bible tells me so
Jesus loves me
Ain't no doubt (ain't no doubt)
So I'm gonna keep on talking about
Oh, yeah"

"Every one of those Sunday sermons
Every time that choir would sing (that choir would sing)
I could hear my Savior calling, telling me how much He loves me
No matter what the world throws at me
I know I'll make it through
All because of those heart stirring, spirit moving Sunday Sermons"

"Devil gon' try and take me out of that church
But you can't take the church out of me
Devil gon' try and take me out of that church
But you can't take the church out of me"

"Devil gon' try and take me out of that church
But you can't take the church out of me
Devil gon' try and take me out of that church
But you can't take the church out of me."

*"For God so loved the world, that He gave His
only begotten Son, that whosoever believeth in
Him should not perish but have everlasting life."*
John 3:16

REFLECTION PAGE

WHAT IS YOUR FIRST REACTION AFTER LISTENING/READING THIS SONG?

DID THIS SONG INSPIRE YOU TO INCREASE YOUR RELATIONSHIP WITH GOD? WHY?

HOW MUCH DOES MUSIC MINISTRY FIT INTO YOUR WORSHIP?

"WHAT A DAY THAT WILL BE"

Written by: Jim Hill

This beautiful gospel hymn was written in the 1950's by Jim Hill. The song is a traditional favorite in churches and immediately motivates congregations to their feet in emotional worship.

As reported in an article with *christianmusicandhymns.com*, Jim Hill talked about his reasoning and motivation for writing the popular favorite. Hill talked of visiting his gravely ill mother-in-law and after leaving her bedside and driving home he wrote the hymn.

Hill talked about how he began to question why God was allowing his mother-in-law to suffer, and as he wondered, the words of Revelations 21:4 came to his mind. The verse in part says, "...God shall wipe away all tears from their eyes: and there shall be no more pain for the former things are passed away."

Hill said that while reflecting on that verse the song came to his mind. The song talks about the day the Lord Jesus Christ will come back to earth and take us to a home where there will be no more suffering or sickness.

"What a day that will be when my Jesus I shall see, I look upon his face, the one who saved me by His grace, when He takes me by the hand and leads me through the promised land....." is a thought each Christian always has in his/her mind about that very first time we come face to face with our precious Savior and taking that first walk with Him through the beauty of heaven.

"There'll be no sorrows there, no more burdens to bear, no more sickness and no more pain....." details the marvelous excitement and realization that we will be in the presence of perfection in all ways with all our friends and family with no problems or worries for all eternity.

"But forever I will be with the one who died for me, what a day, that glorious day will be....." tells us that our journey through life's toils and troubles will be over and we will be with our blessed Lord and Savior Jesus Christ for all eternity.

"What a day that will be
When my Jesus I shall see
And I look upon His face
The One who saved me by His grace
When He takes me by the hand
And leads me through the Promised Land
What a day, glorious day that will be"

"There'll be no sorrows there
No more burdens to bear
No more sickness and no more pain
No more parting over there
But forever I will be
With the one who died for me
What a day, glorious day that will be"

"What a day that will be
When my Jesus I shall see
When I look upon His face
The One who saved me by His grace
When He takes me by the hand
And leads me through the Promised Land
What a day, glorious day that will be"

"Oh what a day that will be

When my Jesus I shall see
When I look upon His face
The One who saved me by His grace
When He takes me by the hand
And leads me through the Promised Land
What a day, glorious day that will be."

*"I will not forget you! See, I have
engraved you on the palms of my
hands; your walls are ever before me."*
Isaiah 49: 15-16 NIV

REFLECTION PAGE

WHAT IS YOUR FIRST REACTION AFTER LISTENING/READING THIS SONG?

DID THIS SONG INSPIRE YOU TO INCREASE YOUR RELATIONSHIP WITH GOD? WHY?

HOW MUCH DOES MUSIC MINISTRY FIT INTO YOUR WORSHIP?

CHAPTER 17

"SWEET BEULAH LAND"

Written by: Squire Parsons, Jr.

"Sweet Beulah Land," was written in 1973 by Squire Parsons, Jr. In an interview by the *Cullman Times,* Parsons, Jr., talked about the song, saying he began writing the lyrics alone in a band room with the words running through his mind. He later composed the music to those lyrics.

Parsons Jr. was born in Newton, West Virginia, in April, 1948. He was introduced to the music business by his father who was a choir director and deacon at Newton Baptist Church. He attended West Virginia Institute of Technology earning a Bachelor of Science degree in music.

Parsons Jr. has been nominated for the *DOVE Award* for male vocalist and songwriter. In 1990, he was awarded the "Marvin Norcross Award", given for devotion to church, family, involvement in community affairs, and contributions to the gospel music industry. In 1999 he was presented with an honorary Doctorate of Humanities by West Virginia Institute of Technology and October 9, 2008, he was inducted into the Southern Gospel Music's "Hall of Fame," in Pigeon Forge, TN.

According to the interview, "Sweet Beulah Land," was not recorded until 1979, after Parsons Jr., had joined the Kingsmen Quartet. By 1981, the song was the number one Southern Gospel Single. The composition also won the *Singing News Fan Awards* for Song of the Year that same year.

The song has been recorded by several other artists over the years including Carroll Roberson, the Chuck Wagon Gang, and the Gaither Homecoming Choir.

Additionally on a personal note, I will never forget the beautiful voice my late father-in-law, Thomas Seth, had and the tears of emotion and joy the congregations at the Church of Christ in Christian Union in New Boston, Ohio, displayed at every Sunday morning service we were privileged to hear him sing that wonderful hymn.

"I'm kind of homesick for a country to which I've never been before, no sad goodbyes will there be spoken for time won't matter anymore..." reflects the thoughts Christians have deep in the back of our minds that periodically comes to the forefront as we go through the various trials and tribulations of life, homesick for our ultimate home.

"Beulah Land (Beulah Land) I'm longing for you, and some day on thee I'll stand, some day we will stand..." illustrates the desire and emotion all true Christians have in our hearts and souls to one glorious day set foot in our heavenly reward.

"I'm looking now, just across the river, to where my faith, shall end in sight, there's just a few more days to labor, then I will take my heavenly flight..." mirrors the river as the time between completing our life in this world and our arrival in the Promised Land.

"I'm kind of homesick for a country
To which I've never been before
No sad goodbyes will there be spoken
For time won't matter anymore"

"Beulah Land (Beulah Land) I'm longing for you
And some day on thee I'll stand, some day we will stand
There my home shall be eternal
Beulah Land, sweet Beulah Land"

"I'm looking now, just across the river
To where my faith, shall end in sight
There's just a few more days to labor
Then I will take my heavenly flight"

"Beulah Land (Beulah Land) I'm longing for you
And some day on thee I'll stand, some day we will stand
There my home shall be eternal
Beulah Land, sweet Beulah Land
Beulah Land, oh it's Beulah Land
Oh Beulah Land, sweet Beulah Land

*"Seek ye first the Kingdom of God, and
His righteousness, and all these things
shall be added unto you."*
Matthew 6:33 KJV

REFLECTION PAGE

WHAT IS YOUR FIRST REACTION AFTER LISTENING/READING THIS SONG?

DID THIS SONG INSPIRE YOU TO INCREASE YOUR RELATIONSHIP WITH GOD? WHY?

HOW MUCH DOES MUSIC MINISTRY FIT INTO YOUR WORSHIP?

CHAPTER 18

"THE OLD RUGGED CROSS"

Written by: George Bennard

Wikipedia reports that "The Old Rugged Cross," was written in 1912 by American evangelist George Bennard. Bennard was a native of Youngstown, Ohio, who went through his conversion at a Salvation Army meeting where he eventually met his wife, and they became brigade leaders later leaving the Salvation Army and joining the Methodist Church.

Bennard became a Methodist evangelist and eventually wrote the first verse of "the Old Rugged Cross" in the fall of 1912. The total version was completed and then performed on June 7, 1913, by a choir of five, accompanied by a guitar in Pokagon, Michigan, at the First Methodist Episcopal Church of Pokagon. Michigan, at the First Methodist Episcopal Church of Pokagon.

The song was published in 1915 and popularized during *Billy Sunday* evangelistic campaigns by two members of Bennard's staff, Homer Rodeheaver and Virginia Asher, who possibly were the first to record it in 1921.

As all who have listened to this beautiful hymn know, the song references the writer's adoration of Christ and His sacrifice on Calvary.

"The Old Rugged Cross" is a routinely sang and much admired Christian hymn popular throughout the world wherever Christianity is present. The song has a unique meaning to Christians as the very title brings immediate attention to the ultimate sacrifice made by our Lord and Savior Jesus Christ.

"On a hill far away stood an old rugged cross, the emblem of suffering and shame, and I love that old cross where the dearest and best, for a world of lost sinners was slain...." indicates the stark cold realization that the most barbaric and unimaginable event in the history of mankind occurred to the only true and pure individual to ever walk on earth.

"So I'll cherish the old rugged cross, till my trophies at last I lay down, I will cling to the old rugged cross, and exchange it some day for a crown..." implies that the sacrifice resulting from the crucifixion, however horrible, will always be remembered until meeting our precious Savior in Heaven.

"To the old rugged cross I will ever be true, it's shame and reproach gladly bear, then He'll call me some day to my home far away, where His glory forever I'll share...." tells us that regardless of the shame and embarrassment this ruthless event reflects on us all, we still look forward to the day we meet in Heaven and give thanks for His love and sacrifice.

"And I'll cherish the old rugged cross, till my trophies at last I lay down, and I will cling to the old rugged cross, and exchange it some day for a crown..." signifies that when it is time for us to make the final journey, we will gladly forget all of life's temporary achievements and only focus on the rewards of life eternal in heaven.

"On a hill far away stood and old rugged cross
The emblem of suffering and shame
And I love that old cross where the dearest and best
For a world of lost sinners was slain"

"So I'll cherish the old rugged cross
Till my trophies at last I lay down
I will cling to the old rugged cross
And exchange it some day for a crown"

"To the old rugged cross will I ever be true
It's shame and reproach gladly bear
Then he'll call me some day to my home far away
Where His glory forever I'll share"

"And I'll cherish the old rugged cross
Till my trophies at last I lay down
And I will cling to the old rugged cross
And exchange it some day for a crown
I will cling to the old rugged cross
And exchange it some day for a crown.

"Everyone who sins breaks the law; in fact, sin is lawlessness. But you know that He appeared so that He might take away our sins. And in Him is no sin. No one who lives in Him keeps on sinning."

1 John 3:4-6 NIV

REFLECTION PAGE

WHAT IS YOUR FIRST REACTION AFTER LISTENING/READING THIS SONG?

DID THIS SONG INSPIRE YOU TO INCREASE YOUR RELATIONSHIP WITH GOD? WHY?

HOW MUCH DOES MUSIC MINISTRY FIT INTO YOUR WORSHIP?

CHAPTER 19

"GREAT IS THY FAITHFULNESS"

Written by: Thomas Chisholm
Music Composed by: William M. Runyan

"Great is Thy Faithfulness," was written in 1923 by Thomas Chisholm and William Runyan later composed music for the hymn and it was eventually published by Hope Publishing Company becoming a popular hit among church groups throughout the country.

The song was given national attention after becoming a favorite of Dr. William Henry Houghton of Moody Bible Institute and with the Reverend Billy Graham who used it at many of his international crusades. Since the middle of the 20th century, it has been the university hymn of Cairn University.

The Gospel Forum in an article on Chisholm, explained he was born in Franklin, Kentucky in 1866. Chisholm was a minister who also worked as an insurance salesman and by the time of his retirement had written over 800 published poems.

George Beverly Shea, one of the regular singers in *the Billy Graham Crusades,* introduced "Great is Thy Faithfulness," to those meetings in Great Britain in 1954. Today it is one of the most popular hymns ever written and is consequently in the *CCL* top 100.

"Great is Thy Faithfulness, O God my Father, there is no shadow of turning with Thee, Thou changest not, Thy compassions, they fail not, as

Thou hast been, Thou forever will be...." reflects that God is and always will be constant in His love and caring for all.

"Great is Thy Faithfulness, great is Thy Faithfulness, morning by morning new mercies I see, all I have needed Thy hand hath provided, Great is Thy faithfulness, Lord unto me...." indicates that each new day brings more mercy and understanding for our mistakes and misguided judgements, by our Lord and Savior.

"Summer and winter and springtime and harvest, sun, moon and stars in their courses above, join with all nature in manifold witness, to Thy Great Faithfulness, mercy and love...." tells all Christians God's love and devotion will be with us every season of our lives.

"Pardon for sin and a peace that endureth, Thine own dear presence to cheer and to guide, strength for today and bright hope for tomorrow, blessings all mine with 10,000 beside...." lets us know that as our Savior died for our sins, we now live with comforting knowledge that even as we live through often difficult times, happiness and love will eventually be ours for all eternity.

"Great is Thy Faithfulness, O God my Father
There is no shadow of turning with Thee
Thou changest not, Thy compassions, they fail not
As Thou hast been, Thou forever will be"

"Great is Thy Faithfulness
Great is Thy faithfulness
Morning by morning new mercies I see
All I have needed Thy hand hath provided
Great is Thy faithfulness, Lord unto me"

"Summer and winter and springtime and harvest
Sun, moon and stars in their courses above
Join with all nature in manifold witness
To Thy great faithfulness, mercy and love"

"Great is Thy Faithfulness
Great is Thy Faithfulness
Morning by morning new mercies I see
All I have needed Thy hand hath provided
Great is Thy faithfulness, Lord unto me"

"Pardon for sin and a peace that endureth
Thine own dear presence to cheer and to guide
Strength for today and bright hope for tomorrow
Blessings all mine with 10,000 beside"

"Great is Thy faithfulness
Great is Thy faithfulness
Morning by morning new mercies I see
Great is Thy faithfulness
Great is Thy faithfulness
Great is Thy faithfulness, Lord, unto me."

*"But this I call to mind, and therefore I have
hope: The steadfast love of the Lord never
ceases; his mercies never come to an end;
they are new every morning; great is your
faithfulness."*

Lamentations 3:21-23

REFLECTION PAGE

WHAT IS YOUR FIRST REACTION AFTER LISTENING/READING THIS SONG?

DID THIS SONG INSPIRE YOU TO INCREASE YOUR RELATIONSHIP WITH GOD? WHY?

HOW MUCH DOES MUSIC MINISTRY FIT INTO YOUR WORSHIP?

CHAPTER 20

"ROOM AT THE CROSS FOR YOU"

Written & Composed by: Ira Forest Stanphill

According to *hymnstudiesblog*, a blog devoted to the study of the background, authors, composers and meaning of hymns, "Room at the Cross for You," was written in 1945 by Ira Forest Stanphill. Stanphill was born February 14, 1914, at Bellview, New Mexico.

Stanphill received his high school and junior high school education while attending Assembly of God, and later received a PhD from Hyles-Anderson College in Hammond, IN. Stanphill began preaching in Arcadia, KS, and in 1936 became minister at a church in Springfield, MO.

One of Stanphill's practices during a church meeting was to produce a new gospel song from suggested titles received from the audience. "Room at the Cross for You," was written as a result of a suggestion by an audience member at one of those Sunday meetings in 1945.

The song first appeared in Stanphill's publication, *Hymntime Harmonies,* eventually being translated into several foreign languages including Spanish, German and Italian. "Room at the Cross for You," was also used by the nationally aired *Revival Time Broadcast,* as its closing theme for many years. Also, the song appeared in the 1977 *Special Sacred Selections,* 1978/1983 *Church Gospel Songs and Hymns* and the 2010 *Songs for Worship and Praise.*

"Room at the Cross for You," focuses attention on the blessings of the cross. The song reminds us about the peace which we can have through the blood of the cross.

"The cross upon which Jesus died, is a shelter in which we can hide; and its grace so free is sufficient for me, and deep is its fountain as wide as the sea...." explains the cross as a symbol of the sacrifice Jesus gave for us to free us of sin through His overwhelming grace.

"There's room at the cross for you, there's room at the cross for you, though millions have come, there's still room for one, yes there's room at the cross for you...." implies that our Savior's sacrifice was not just for some but for everyone at any time, all we have to do is ask.

"Though millions have found him a friend, and have turned from the sins they have sinned, the Savior still waits to open the gates, and welcomes a sinner before it's too late..." recognizes that although generations have been saved by grace, millions more will always have the opportunity.

"The hand of my Savior is strong, and the love of my Savior is long, through sunshine or rain, through loss or in gain, the blood flows from Calvary to cleanse every stain..." emphasizes the great strength, love and caring our Lord and Savior has for each of us will always be present regardless of what challenges or difficulties may come.

"The cross upon which Jesus died,
Is a shelter in which we can hide;
And it's grace so free is sufficient for me
And deep is its fountain, as wide as the sea"

"There's Room at the Cross for You,"
There's Room at the Cross for You,
Though millions have come, there's still
room for one
Yes, There's Room at the Cross for You"

"Though millions have found Him a friend
And have turned from the sins they
have sinned,
The Savior still waits to open the gates
And welcome a sinner before its too late"

"There's Room at the Cross for You,
There's Room at the Cross for You
Though millions have come, there's still
room for one,
Yes, there's room at the cross for you"

"The hand of my Savior is strong,
And the love of my Savior is long,
Through sunshine and rain, through loss
or in rain,
The blood flows from Calvary to
Cleanse every stain"

"There's Room at the Cross for You,
There's Room at the Cross for You,
Though millions have come, there's still
room for one,
Yes, There's Room at the Cross for You."

*"For it pleased the Father...having
made peace through the blood of
His Cross..."*

Colossians 1:19-20

REFLECTION PAGE

WHAT IS YOUR FIRST REACTION AFTER LISTENING/READING THIS SONG?

DID THIS SONG INSPIRE YOU TO INCREASE YOUR RELATIONSHIP WITH GOD? WHY?

HOW MUCH DOES MUSIC MINISTRY FIT INTO YOUR WORSHIP?

CHAPTER 21

"MIGHTY TO SAVE"

Written by: Ben Felding, Reuben Morgan
Song by Hillsong Publishing

Wikipedia reports that "Mighty to Save," is from the album *Mighty to Save* with the rights to the song registered to Hillsong Publishing.

Recorded live in March 2006, at the Sydney Entertainment Center in Sydney, Australia, it won the Worship Song of the Year at the *Dove Awards* in 2009.

As reported in *Christian Song Meaning (christiansongmeaning.wordpress. com)* the meaning of "Mighty to Save," is that our God can do everything in His hands. Although we are in a world that is full of lies and darkness, God always provides light and shines through the dark.

Pray to the Lord, follow, surrender, and believe in Him and for sure He will bless you no matter what you are going through, God truly is mighty to save, because He truly loves us, has ability to defeat death and is full of grace and mercy.

"Mighty to Save," has quickly become one of the most popular contemporary Christian songs performed by church bands and choirs throughout the United States.

"Everyone needs compassion, a love that's never failing, let mercy fall on me, everyone needs forgiveness, the kindness of a Savior, Hope of nations...."talks of the very gifts God bestows on each of us through His divine grace.

"Savior, He can move the mountains, my God is mighty to save, He is mighty to save, forever author of salvation, He rose and conquered the grave, Jesus conquered the grave...." speaks of the very awesome power and love our Savior has for us.

"So take me as You find me, all my tears and failures, fill my life again, I give my life to follow, everything I believe in, and now I surrender (I surrender)...." represents the type of prayer each of us offers up when we willfully and faithfully ask God to save our souls and forgive our sins for His love and kindness by accepting Jesus Christ as our personal Lord and Savior.

"Shine your light and let the whole world see, we're singing for the glory of the risen King, Jesus shine Your light and let the whole world see, we're singing for the glory of the risen King...." is reference to us asking God to show all of us that Jesus Christ is the light and the way to a blessed salvation.

"Everyone needs compassion
A love that's never failing, let mercy fall on me
Everyone needs forgiveness
The kindness of a Savior, the Hope of nations"

"Savior, He can move the mountains
My God is mighty to save
He is mighty to save
Forever, author of Salvation
He rose and conquered the grave
Jesus conquered the grave"

"So take me as You find me
All my fears and failures
Fill my life again
I give my life to follow
Everything I believe in
And now I surrender (I surrender)"

"Savior, He can move the mountains
My God is mighty to save

He is mighty to save
Forever, author of Salvation
He rose and conquered the grave
Jesus conquered the grave"

"Savior, He can move the mountains
My God is mighty to save
He is mighty to save
Forever, author of Salvation
He rose and conquered the grave
Jesus conquered the grave"

"Shine Your light and let the whole world see
We're singing for the glory of the risen King, Jesus
Shine Your light and let the whole world see
We're singing for the glory of the risen King"

"Savior, He can move the mountains
My God is mighty to save
He is mighty to save
Forever, author of salvation
He rose and conquered the grave
Jesus conquered the grave"

"Shine Your light and let the whole world see
We're singing for the glory of the risen King, Jesus
Shine your light and let the whole world see
We're singing for the glory of the risen King
Shine Your light and let the whole world see
We're singing for the glory of the risen King, Jesus"

"Shine Your light and let the whole world see
We're singing for the glory of the risen King
Shine Your light and let the whole world see
We're singing for the glory of the risen King, Jesus
Shine Your light and let the whole world see,
We're singing for the glory of the risen King."

"But even so, you love me! You are holding my right hand! You will keep on guiding me all my life with your wisdom and counsel, and afterwards receive me into the glories of heaven!

Psalm 73:23-24 TLB

REFLECTION PAGE

WHAT IS YOUR FIRST REACTION AFTER LISTENING/READING THIS SONG?

DID THIS SONG INSPIRE YOU TO INCREASE YOUR RELATIONSHIP WITH GOD? WHY?

HOW MUCH DOES MUSIC MINISTRY FIT INTO YOUR WORSHIP?

"Jesus Paid It All"

Written by: Elvina M. Hall
Music by: John Grape

"Jesus Paid it All," was written in 1865 by Elvina M. Hall and music written by John Grape. The song was then initially published in *"Sabbath Carols,"* and has been a church favorite ever since.

Country Thang Daily, talks in its article on this great Christian song that it celebrates the total sufficiency of Christ's sacrifice on the cross to save us from sin. The article discusses how the meaning of the cross turns our minds to salvation and how God's greatest sacrifice was for the love of mankind.

The overall theme of "Jesus Paid it All," is that our sin debt is indeed paid and was paid by the blood of Jesus Christ on the cross. Jesus's last words on the cross before dying were, "It is finished," which tells us that His death wiped away our debt forever and opened a way for all of us to spend eternity together in heaven if we so choose the opportunity.

The realization that God, through His grace, displayed this unmeasurable love for each of us, is a remarkable awareness that should be the motivation to move forward in life following the Word of God and a life of sanctification.

"I hear the Savior say, Thy strength indeed is small, child of weakness watch and pray, find in me thine all in all......" refers to the Savior as the only real strength and power, with prayer being the sole tool for asking for His divine attention and assistance.

"Jesus paid it all, all to Him I owe, sin had left a crimson stain, He washed it white as snow..." lets us know that Jesus died to pay for the sins of mankind and created a pathway to eternal salvation.

"Lord, now indeed I find, Thy power and Thine alone, came and changed the lepers spots, and it melt the heart of stone...." describes how we have realized that it is the power of God that is able to change attitudes and actions of nonbelievers.

"And when before the throne, I stand in Him complete, Jesus died my soul to save, my lips shall still repeat..." is our testimony that our faith, love and total loyalty is to God who sacrificed His only Son for our salvation.

"Jesus paid it all, all to Him I owe, Sin had left a crimson stain, He washed it white as snow...." tells us we owe our salvation to the ultimate sacrifice God made and the crimson stain of blood washed away the dirt of sin.

"Oh praise Him, Oh praise Him, Oh Praise Him...." is thanks and reflects gratitude.

"You change my destiny God, Ah You change my life, I praise You, I praise You, yes...." is our realization of what Christ's death on the cross meant for us.

"I hear the Savior say
Thy strength indeed is small
Child of weakness watch and pray
Find in me thine all in all"

"Jesus paid it all
All to Him I owe
Sin had left a crimson stain
He washed it white as snow"

"Lord, now indeed I find
Thy power and thine alone
Came and changed the lepers spots
And it melt the heart of stone"

"Jesus paid it all
All to Him I owe
Sin had left a crimson stain
He washed it white as snow"

"And when before the throne
I stand in Him complete
Jesus died my soul to save
My lips shall still repeat"

"Jesus paid it all
All to Him I owe
Sin had left a crimson stain
He washed it white as snow"

"Jesus paid it all
All to Him I owe
Sin had left a crimson stain
He washed it white as snow
He washed it white as snow
He washed it white as snow"

"Oh, praise the one who paid my debt
And rises life up from the dead
Oh, praise the one who paid my debt
And rises life up from the dead
Oh, praise the one who paid my debt
And rises life up from the dead
Oh, praise the one who paid my debt
And rises life up from the dead
Oh, praise the one who paid my debt
And rises life up from the dead
Oh, praise the one who paid my debt
And rises life up from the dead"

"Oh praise Him
Oh praise Him
Oh praise Him
Oh praise Him
Ohhh"

"You change my destiny God
Ah you change my life
I praise You, I praise You, yes"

"Oh, praise the one who paid my debt
And rises life up from the dead
Oh, praise the one who paid my debt
And rises life up from the dead
Oh, praise the one who paid my debt
And rises life up from the dead
Oh, praise the one who paid my debt
And rises life up from the dead"

"Jesus paid it all
All to Him I owe
Sin had left a crimson stain
He washed it white as snow"

"Jesus paid it all
All to Him I owe
Sin had left a crimson stain
He washed it white as snow"

*"Let us practice loving each other, for
love comes from God and those who
are loving and kind show that they
are the children of God, and that they
are getting to know Him better."*

1 John 4:7 TLB

REFLECTION PAGE

WHAT IS YOUR FIRST REACTION AFTER LISTENING/READING THIS SONG?

DID THIS SONG INSPIRE YOU TO INCREASE YOUR RELATIONSHIP WITH GOD? WHY?

HOW MUCH DOES MUSIC MINISTRY FIT INTO YOUR WORSHIP?

CHAPTER 23

"OVERCOME"

Words and Music by: Jon Egan

"Overcome," has been performed under alternative titles such as, *We Will Overcome, Savior, Worthy of Honor and Glory* and *Seated Above*.

According to the blog, *strongworshipsongs,* by Pastor Scott Martz, the song was written in 2007 as response to a horrible incident at his Colorado church in which a mad gunman shot six innocent church goers killing two of them in their church parking lot. Jeremy Camp, then featured the song on his *Worship Project* album in August 2010.

The lyrics of the song are very Christ-centered and emphasize the fact that God's perfect son suffered and died to pay for the sins of all mankind but then overcame death on the third day and now lives.

This truly beautiful and moving song, coming from the depths of tragedy serves as a source of motivation and inspiration to Christians everywhere.

"Seated above, enthroned in the Father's love, destined to die, poured out for all mankind, God's only Son, perfect and spotless one, He never sinned but suffered as if He did....."is our description of Jesus Christ sitting in His splendor at the right hand of God.

"Savior, Savior worthy of honor and glory, worthy of all our praise, You overcame, Jesus, awesome in power forever, Awesome and great is Your name, You overcame..." is the appreciation and thanks we have for all He overcame for us because of His love for us.

"All authority, every victory is Yours...." is our recognition of the goodness, glory and power of our beloved Savior.

"We will overcome by the blood of the Lamb, and the word of our testimony, everyone overcome, we will overcome, by the blood of the Lamb and the word of our testimony, everyone overcome...." indicates the blood sacrificed on the cross made our salvation possible and our realization that thanks is not nearly enough.

"Seated above, enthroned in the Father's love
Destined to die, poured out for all mankind
God's only Son, perfect and spotless one
He never sinned but suffered as if He did"

"All authority
Every victory is Yours
All authority
Every victory is Yours"

"Savior
Savior, worthy of honor and glory
Worthy of all our praise, You overcame
Jesus, awesome in power forever
Awesome and great is Your name, You overcame"

"Power in hand speaking the Father's plan
You're send us out, light in this broken land"

"All authority
Every victory is Yours"

"Savior, worthy of honor and glory
Worthy of all our praise, You overcame, You overcame
Jesus, awesome in power forever
Awesome and great is Your name, You overcame, yeah"

"We will overcome by the blood of the Lamb
and the word of our testimony, everyone overcome"

"We will overcome by the blood of the Lamb
And the word of our testimony, everyone overcome"

"We will overcome by the blood of the Lamb
And the word of our testimony, everyone overcome"

"We will overcome by the blood of the Lamb
And the word of our testimony, everyone overcome"

"Savior, worthy of honor and glory
Worthy of all our praise, You overcame, You overcame Jesus
Jesus, awesome in power forever,
Awesome and great is Your name, You overcame"

"You overcame (You overcame)
Jesus (You overcame)
You overcame (You overcame)
You overcame"

"Savior, worthy of honor and glory
Worthy of all our praise, You overcame, You overcame,
Jesus, awesome in power forever
Awesome and great is Your name (Your name), You overcame
You overcame
Jesus
You overcame"

*"You will keep in perfect peace Him'
whose mind is steadfast, because He
trusts in you. Trust in the LORD
forever, for the LORD, for the LORD, is the
Rock eternal."*

Isaiah 26:3 NIV

REFLECTION PAGE

WHAT IS YOUR FIRST REACTION AFTER LISTENING/READING THIS SONG?

DID THIS SONG INSPIRE YOU TO INCREASE YOUR RELATIONSHIP WITH GOD? WHY?

HOW MUCH DOES MUSIC MINISTRY FIT INTO YOUR WORSHIP?

CHAPTER 24

"BLESSED BE YOUR NAME"

Written by: Matt Redman and Beth Redman

"Blessed Be Your Name," was written by Matt and Beth Redman and performed by Matt Redman. Wikipedia reports that the song track appeared on Matt Redman's 2002 album, *Where Angels Fear to Thread,* on the Worship Together label.

The song was performed in 2003 by the South African Christian band *Tree63,* and that version went to number 2 on the US Billboard Christian Songs chart and stayed 68 weeks.

The song later appeared on Matt Redman's 2005 album, *Blessed Be Your Name: The Songs of Matt Redman Vol. 1,* which was released on Survivor Records.

In 2005, "Blessed Be Your Name," won the *GMA Dove Award,* for Worship Song of the Year. The song continues to be one of the most popular contemporary Christian songs of our time and motivates and inspires world-wide.

"Blessed be Your name, in the land that is plentiful, where the streams of abundance flow, blessed be Your name..." signifies that the glory of God spreads throughout our land and He is responsible for all that is good.

"Blessed be Your name, when I'm found in the desert place, though I walk through the wilderness, blessed be Your name..." says you lead me safely through the dangerous places and let me know by believing in You I will never be alone.

"Every blessing You pour out, I'll turn back to praise, when the darkness closes in Lord, still I will say, blessed be the name of the Lord, blessed be Your name..." implies for every blessing I have ever received or ever will receive, I will constantly give you thanks and praise.

"Blessed be Your name, when the sun is shining down on me, when the world's 'all as it should be,' blessed be Your name..." signifies that for all the credit and all the success, I know the glory goes all to God.

"Blessed be Your name, on the road marked with suffering, though there's pain in the offering, blessed be Your name..." shows that during the bad times of challenges I know you will be leading me.

"You give and take away, You give and take away, my heart will choose to say, Lord blessed be Your name..." recognizes that although everything in life won't be easy, God has a purpose and will guide our lives if we let Him.

"Blessed be Your name
In the land that is plentiful
Where Your streams of abundance flow
Blessed be Your name"

"Blessed be Your name
When I'm found in the desert place
Though I walk through the wilderness
Blessed be Your name"

"Every blessing You pour out I'll
Turn back to praise
When the darkness closes in Lord
Still I will say,
Blessed be the name of the Lord
Blessed be Your name
Blessed be the name of the Lord
Blessed be Your glorious name"

"Blessed be Your name
When the sun is shining down on me
When the world's 'all as it should be'
Blessed be Your name"

"Blessed be Your name
On the road marked with suffering
Though there's pain in the offering
Blessed be Your name"

"Every blessing You pour out I'll
Turn back to praise
When the darkness closes in Lord
Still I'll say
Blessed be the name of the Lord
Blessed be Your name
Blessed be the name of the Lord
Blessed be Your glorious name"

"Blessed be the name of the Lord
Blessed be Your name
Blessed be the name of the Lord
Blessed be Your glorious name"

"You give and take away
You give and take away
My heart will choose to say
Lord blessed be Your name"

"Blessed be the name of the Lord
Blessed be Your name
Blessed be the name of the Lord
Blessed be Your glorious name"

"Blessed by the name of the Lord
Blessed be Your name
Blessed be the name of the Lord
Blessed be Your glorious name."

"God is faithful, He will not let you be
tempted beyond what you can bear.
But when you are tempted, He will
also provide a way out so that you
can stand up under it."

1 Corinthians 10:13 NIV

REFLECTION PAGE

WHAT IS YOUR FIRST REACTION AFTER LISTENING/READING THIS SONG?

DID THIS SONG INSPIRE YOU TO INCREASE YOUR RELATIONSHIP WITH GOD? WHY?

HOW MUCH DOES MUSIC MINISTRY FIT INTO YOUR WORSHIP?

CHAPTER 25

"WHO YOU SAY I AM"

Written by: Reuben Morgan and Ben Fielding
Performed by: Hillsong Worship

"Who You Say I Am," which is performed by Hillsong Worship, was released on June 15, 2018, as the first single from their 26th live album, *There is More*, by Hillsong Music Australia and Capitol Christian Music Group (Wikipedia).

On October 19, 2018, Hillsong Worship released an instrumental version of "Who You Say I Am," in the instrumental album, *There is More: Instrumental*. The song was nominated for Top Christian Song at the *2019 Billboard Music Awards*.

In a January 2019 article in *Churchfront,* Kaylee Gosselin talked about the song's inspiration coming from *John 8*. "One the song's most repeated lines, 'who the sun sets free is free indeed,' sounds familiar to many church goers, likely because it's a direct quote from Jesus (John 8:36)"

"Who You Say I Am," is a popular motivational song for Sunday morning church, being easy to sing, repetitive simplistic in nature, and the song's theme is quick to understand as Ben Fielding says, "we immediately understand what our identity is...we are each a child of God." Freedom is the reality for anyone whose identity is a child of God. "It's the key idea of Jesus' announcement in *John 8,* "Who the Son sets free is free indeed..." Jesus has the power to set us free from whatever or however bad our sin may be.

The song in essence describes everyone's need for a Savior and the Father's grace in providing Jesus Christ to pave the way for our salvation.

"Who am I that the highest King, would welcome me, I was lost but He brought me in, Oh His love for me, Oh His love for me...." represents the wonder we all have as to why God would bring a lost, former non-believer into His Kingdom with love.

"Who the Son sets free, Oh is free indeed, I'm a child of God, Yes I am..." tells us anyone God frees from the chains of sin will stay free and be protected by the love of God.

"Free at last, He has ransomed me, His grace runs deep, while I was a slave to sin, Jesus died for me, Yes He died for me..." reflects how God let His Son die for us while we were sinners and then because of His unconditional love gave us a way to salvation thru His divine grace.

"In my Father's house, there's a place for me, I'm a child of God, Yes I am..." implies that Jesus has indeed prepared an eternal home for us in heaven.

"I'm chosen, not forsaken, I am who You say I am, You are for me, not against me, I am who I say I am, I am who I say I am...." reminds us we are chosen by God who always has and always will love us.

"Who am I that the highest King
Would welcome me?
I was lost but He brought me in
Oh His love for me
Oh His love for me"

"Who the Sun sets free
Oh is free indeed
I'm a child of God
Yes I am"

"Free at last
He has ransomed me
His grace runs deep
While I was a slave to sin
Jesus died for me
Yes, He died for me"

"Who the Son sets free
Oh is free indeed
I'm a child of God
Yes I am"

"In my Father's house
There's a place for me
I'm a child of God
Yes I am"

"I am chosen, not forsaken
I am who You say I am
You are for me, not against me
I am who You say I am"

"I am chosen, not forsaken
I am who You say I am
You are for me, not against me
I am who You say I am"

"I am chosen, not forsaken
I am who You say I am
You are for me, not against me
I am who You say I am
I am who You say I am"

"Who the sun sets free
Oh is free indeed
I'm a child of God
Yes I am"

"In my Father's house
There's a place for me
I'm a child of God
Yes I am"

"In my Father's house
There's a place for me
I'm a child of God
Yes I am"

*"If the Son therefore shall make
you free, ye shall be free indeed."*

John 8:36

REFLECTION PAGE

WHAT IS YOUR FIRST REACTION AFTER LISTENING/READING THIS SONG?

DID THIS SONG INSPIRE YOU TO INCREASE YOUR RELATIONSHIP WITH GOD? WHY?

HOW MUCH DOES MUSIC MINISTRY FIT INTO YOUR WORSHIP?

CHAPTER 26

"IN THE SWEET BY AND BY"

Written by: S. Fillmore Bennett
Music by: Joseph P. Webster

It's doubtful anyone who has spent any time listening to Christian music has not heard "In the Sweet By and By," at least one time and probably several. First published in 1868, written by S. Fillmore Bennett and music written by Joseph P. Webster, the song has a distinct and popular flavor which motivates everyone present to join in singing from the congregation to the chorus.

Wikipedia talks of the song being extremely popular in the 19th century. In 1885, crowds of admirers reportedly sang the hymn at a railway station to departing American temperance evangelists Mary Greenleaf Clement Leavitt of the *Woman's Christian Temperance Union* and *Blue Ribbon Army* representative R.T. Booth.

Over the years recording artists Elvis Presley, Louis Armstrong, Johnny Cash, Glen Campbell, Dolly Parton, Willie Nelson, Loretta Lynn and Kenny Rogers have offered their renditions of this Christian classic. Additionally, the *Salvation Army* has popularized the song and it is often sung at Army funeral services.

As reported in *hymnstudiesblog*, among hymnbooks published by members of the Lord's church for use in churches of Christ, the song appeared in the 1921 *Great Songs of the Church No. 1* and the 1937 *Great*

Songs of the Church No. 2. and various other publications, most recently the 2010 *Songs for Worship and Praise,* in addition to *Hymns for Worship* and *Sacred Selections.*

"There's a land that is fairer than day, and by faith we can see it afar, for the Father waits over the way, to prepare us a dwelling place there...." implies that only thru faith can we see our eternal home and only thru grace will we be welcomed by God.

"In the sweet by and by, we shall meet on that beautiful shore, in the sweet by and by, we shall meet on that beautiful shore...." tells us we will eventually meet our Lord and Savior at the beautiful gates of Heaven.

"We shall sing on that beautiful shore, the melodious songs of the blessed, and our spirit shall sorrow no more, not a sign for the blessing of rest...." reminds us that as we meet in Heaven our precious Savior, no more suffering, sickness or pain will ever again hamper our spirit.

"There's a land that is fairer than day
And by faith we can see it afar
For the Father waits over the way
To prepare us a dwelling place there"

"In the sweet by and by
We shall meet on that beautiful shore
In the sweet by and by
We shall meet on that beautiful shore"

"We shall sing on that beautiful shore
The melodious songs of the blessed
And our spirit shall sorrow no more
Not a sign for the blessing of rest"

"In the sweet by and by
We shall meet on that beautiful shore
In the sweet by and by
We shall meet on the beautiful shore"

"In the sweet by and by
We shall meet on that beautiful shore
In the sweet by and by
We shall meet on that beautiful shore"

"In the sweet by and by
In the sweet by and by, oh"

> *"So I commend the enjoyment of life,*
> *because nothing is better for a man*
> *under the sun than to eat and drink*
> *and be glad. Then joy will*
> *accompany him in his work all the*
> *days of the life God has given him*
> *under the sun."*
>
> Ecclesiastes 8:15 NIV

REFLECTION PAGE

WHAT IS YOUR FIRST REACTION AFTER LISTENING/READING THIS SONG?

DID THIS SONG INSPIRE YOU TO INCREASE YOUR RELATIONSHIP WITH GOD? WHY?

HOW MUCH DOES MUSIC MINISTRY FIT INTO YOUR WORSHIP?

CHAPTER 27

"ARE YOU WASHED IN THE BLOOD?"

Written by: Elisha Hoffman

"Are You Washed in the Blood?," as reported by *Godtube* was written by Elisha Hoffman in 1878. The song asks the question, "have you been restored by the love and power of Jesus Christ?" which is a powerful question to all who hear it about their personal commitment to the Lord.

Hoffman, who became a preacher, graduating from Union Seminary, was assigned to preach in Napoleon, Ohio, and in 1872, had composed over 2000 hymns and edited over 50 song books. He grew up singing hymns in church and was eventually ordained as a Presbyterian minister. After pastoring churches in Cleveland and Grafton, Ohio in the 1880s, he moved to Benton Harbor, Michigan, and eventually finished his ministry in Chicago, Illinois.

Wikipedia, in discussing Hoffman, talks of his views on a hymn as a "lyric poem, reverently and devotionally conceived, which is designed to be sung and which expresses the worshipper's attitude toward God or God's purpose in our lives. It should be simple, genuinely emotional, spiritual in quality, and its ideas so direct and so immediately apparent as to unify a congregation while singing it."

It goes without saying that Hoffman was an expert at the motivation of Christians to intensify their faith through gospel music, particularly

MICHAEL E. PAYTON, MA

congregational music and at the same time motivate non-believers to the joy and peace that comes from accepting Christ as Lord and Savior.

"Have you been to Jesus for the cleansing power, are you washed in the blood of the Lamb? Are you fully trusting in His grace this hour, are you washed in the blood of the Lamb?...." asks if you have been saved by the blood spilled by Jesus Christ on the cross: have you been saved?

"Are you washed in the blood, in the soul cleansing blood of the Lamb? Are your garments spotless? Are they white as snow, are you washed in the blood of the Lamb?...." begs the question "have you given your life to Jesus and been forgiven for all sins?"

"Are you walking daily by the Savior's side, are you washed in the blood of the Lamb? Do you rest each moment in the Crucified, are you washed in the blood of the Lamb...." is saying, "Do you follow the Lord, do you follow His commandments and His laws?"

"When the Bridegroom cometh will your robes be white, are you washed in the blood of the Lamb? Will your soul be ready for the mansions bright, and be washed by the blood of the Lamb?...." wants you to decide if you are ready to go to Heaven when Jesus returns?

"Lay aside the garments that are stained with sin, and be washed in the blood of the Lamb? There's a fountain flowing for the soul unclean, O be washed in the blood of the Lamb!...." simply but most importantly says, "ask for forgiveness, repent and accept Jesus Christ as your personal Lord and Savior."

"Have you been to Jesus for the cleansing power?
Are you washed in the blood of the Lamb?
Are you fully trusting in His grace this hour?
Are you washed in the blood of the Lamb?"

"Are you washed in the blood
In the sould cleansing blood of the Lamb?
Are your garments spotless? Are they white as snow?
Are you washed in the blood of the Lamb?"

"Are you walking daily by the Savior's side?
Are you washed in the blood of the Lamb?
Do you rest each moment in the Crucified?
Are you washed in the blood of the Lamb?"

"When the Bridegroom cometh will your robes be white?
Are you washed in the blood of the Lamb?
Will your soul be ready for the mansions bright,
And be washed in the blood of the Lamb?"

"Lay aside the garments that are stained with sin,
And be washed in the blood of the Lamb;
There's a fountain flowing for the soul unclean,
O be washed in the blood of the Lamb!"

"Because of the Lord's great love
we are not consumed, for His
compassions never fail. They are
new every morning; great is Your
faithfulness."
Lamentations 3:22-23 NIV

REFLECTION PAGE

WHAT IS YOUR FIRST REACTION AFTER LISTENING/READING THIS SONG?

DID THIS SONG INSPIRE YOU TO INCREASE YOUR RELATIONSHIP WITH GOD? WHY?

HOW MUCH DOES MUSIC MINISTRY FIT INTO YOUR WORSHIP?

CHAPTER 28

"WHAT A FRIEND WE HAVE IN JESUS"

Written by: Joseph M. Scriven
Music by: Charles Crozat Converse

"What a Friend We Have in Jesus," although written as a poem in 1855 by Joseph M. Scriven, is still today considered a popular contemporary hymn. The music for the song was written by Charles Crozat Converse in 1868. *Wikipedia* reports that the song was originally published by Scriven anonymously and he only started receiving full credit in the 1880s.

KidTunz, in an article by Aria, tells the story that "What a Friend We Have in Jesus," depicts a rich understanding of God forged through times of loss and loneliness. Scriven experienced a life of many losses, including the tragic deaths of two fiancées over a period of several years. Throughout the struggles and loss, he continued to find comfort and strength in his faith and nearness to God who he described as his closest friend.

The words Scriven uses in the song indicate to us that although our lives are challenging and many times painful, we do have someone with us that is a closer friend than any human being could ever be and will always be with us giving support and love. Knowing we have an ever-lasting friend, ready to forgive us of any misdeed, share our joys and feel our pain, guide us safely through the pathways of evil and showing us the way to paradise is motivation and inspiration we can never get anywhere else.

"What a friend we have in Jesus, all our sins and griefs to bear, what a privilege to carry everything to God in prayer...." tells us how privileged we should feel knowing we have someone we can take any problem to and it will be solved.

"O what peace we often forfeit, O what needless pain we bear, all because we do not carry everything to God in prayer....." reminds us that refusing to accept Christ is a refusal for peace, good health and a happy, healthy, loving life with a future in Heaven.

"Have we trials and temptations, is there trouble anywhere, we should never be discouraged, take it to the Lord in prayer. Can we find a friend so faithful who will all our sorrows share, Jesus knows our every weakness, take it to the Lord in prayer...." says no matter what challenges and obstacles we face, having the Lord on our side, able to share our joys and pain, giving us the divine counsel we need, is invaluable friendship.

"Are we weak and heavy laden, cumbered with a load of care...." tells us that no matter what our sorrows or problems are, none are too difficult for our greatest friend and Savior.

"What a friend we have in Jesus,
All our sins and griefs to bear!
What a privilege to carry
Everything to God in prayer!"

"O what peace we often forfeit, O
What needless pain we bear,
All because we do not carry
Everything to God in prayer."

"Have we trials and temptations?
Is there trouble anywhere?
We should never be
Discouraged, take it to the Lord
In prayer."

"Can we find a friend so faithful
Who will all our sorrows share?
Jesus knows our every
Weakness; take it to the Lord in
Prayer."

"Are we weak and heavy laden,
cumbered with a load of care?"

"Precious Savior, still our refuge,
Take it to the Lord in prayer.
Do your friends dispise, forsake
You? Take it to the Lord in
Prayer!
In His arms He'll take and shield
You, you will find a solace there."

> *"Be beautiful inside, in your hearts,*
> *with the lasting charm of a gentle and*
> *quiet spirit that is so precious to God."*
>
> 1 Peter 3:4 TLB

REFLECTION PAGE

WHAT IS YOUR FIRST REACTION AFTER LISTENING/READING THIS SONG?

DID THIS SONG INSPIRE YOU TO INCREASE YOUR RELATIONSHIP WITH GOD? WHY?

HOW MUCH DOES MUSIC MINISTRY FIT INTO YOUR WORSHIP?

"IT IS WELL WITH MY SOUL"

Written by: Horatio Gates Spafford
Music Written by: Philip Bliss

"It is Well with My Soul," as reported in *Godtube*, was written by Horatio Gates Spafford with music composed by Philip Bliss. The song was first published in 1876, and throughout the years since has been a center piece in Sunday morning church services.

As pointed out in an article by *American Songwriter, the Craft and Music,* heartbreak gives birth to great songs: love lost, loved ones missed, and even tragedies elicit the emotions that can best be expressed in the medium of music. These songs move listeners and stir up memories bringing about feelings of nostalgia or melancholy, that sort of sadness that leaves us feeling better and "It is Well with My Soul," is one such song that ignites these emotions.

Due to tragedy and loss, Spafford eventually wrote the words to "It is Well with My Soul," as his heart turned to the faithfulness of God in the midst of loss and the work of Jesus to rescue sinners.

The hymn does not diminish or gloss over pain and tragedy but rather proclaims that God is present in them and greater than them. The lyrics and music have gone unchanged in the 140+ years and is one of the most beloved, motivational, and inspirational Christian songs in our country.

"When peace like a river attendeth my way, when sorrows like sea billows roll, whatever my lot, Thou hast taught me to say, it is well with my soul....," tells us we are secure in our faith, knowing we have a loving, caring Savior, at peace with our lives no matter what challenges come our way.

"It is well (it is well) with my soul (with my soul), it is well, it is well with my soul....," describes the feeling of peace and confidence I will have throughout my life knowing I am and will always be a child of God.

"Though Satan should buffet, though trials should come, let this blest assurance control, that Christ (yes He has) has regarded my helpless estate, and has shed His own blood for my soul,..." reflects our belief that no matter what Satan throws our way, no matter what trials and tribulations come our way, our faith will let us overcome.

"My sin, oh the bliss of this glorious thought (the thought), my sin, not in part, but the while (every bit, every bit, all of it), is nailed to the cross, and I bear it no more (yes), praise the Lord, praise the Lord, O my soul...." says our sins were paid for in blood on the cross by our beloved Savior.

"And Lord, haste the day when my faith shall be sight, the clouds be rolled back as a scroll..." tells us the day the Lord returns we will have praise in our souls knowing we will be with our Lord and Savior for all eternity.

"When peace like a river attendeth my way
When sorrows like sea billows roll
Whatever my lot, Thou hast taught me to say
It is well, it is well with my soul"

"It is well (it is well) with my soul (with my soul)
It is well, it is well with my soul"

"Though Satan should buffet, though trials should come
Let this blest assurance control
That Christ (yes He has) has regarded my helpless estate
And has shed His own blood for my soul"

"My sin, oh the bliss of this glorious thought (the thought)
My sin, not in part, but the whole (every bit, every bit, all of it)
Is nailed to the cross, and I bear it no more (yes)
Praise the Lord, praise the Lord, O my soul"

"It is well (it is well) with my soul, (with my soul)
It is well, it is well with my soul (sing it is well)"

"It is well (it is well) with my soul (with my soul)
It is well, it is well with my soul"

"And Lord, haste the day when my faith shall be sight
The clouds be rolled back as a scroll"

"The trump shall resound, and the Lord shall descend
Even so, it is well with my soul"

"It is well, (it is well) with my soul (with my soul)
It is well, it is well with my soul (because of you, Jesus, it is well)"

"It is well (it is well) with my soul (with my soul)
It is well with my soul."

*"Be kind and compassionate to one
another, forgiving each other, just as
in Christ God forgave you."*
Ephesians 4:32 NIV

REFLECTION PAGE

WHAT IS YOUR FIRST REACTION AFTER LISTENING/READING THIS SONG?

DID THIS SONG INSPIRE YOU TO INCREASE YOUR RELATIONSHIP WITH GOD? WHY?

HOW MUCH DOES MUSIC MINISTRY FIT INTO YOUR WORSHIP?

CHAPTER 30

"WHEN THE ROLL IS CALLED UP YONDER"

Written by: James Milton Black
Music by: James Milton Black

Based on *Thessalonians 4,* "When the Roll is Called Up Yonder," is one of the most well-known and well-loved Christian songs of our time. The hymn was written in 1893, music and words, by James Milton Black. The song's lyrics were first published in a collection called, *Songs of the Soul,* and has been translated into 14 languages and sung by countless denominations.

Black was a member of Methodist Episcopal Church in Williamsport, Pennsylvania. *Wikipedia* tells us Black wrote several other hymns including, "Come, Oh Come to Me," "The Day of all Days," and "We Shall Reign with Him in Glory."

"When the Roll is Called Up Yonder," is inspired by the *Book of Life* mentioned in the Bible. There are more than 500 different versions available and by artists such as Loretta Lynn, Johnny Cash, Jim Nabors and Willie Nelson.

Perhaps one of the song's most historic moments came in 1945 when British Prime Minister Winston Churchill quoted the hymn in response to a question about when the Big Three (Churchill, Stalin, Roosevelt) were going to meet. *The Winnipeg Free Press, stated* in part, "Mr. Churchill replied he did not know, but 'When the Roll is Called Up Yonder', I'll be there."

"When the trumpet of the Lord shall sound and shall be no more, and the morning breaks eternal bright and fair, when the saved diverse shall gather over on the other shore, and the roll is called up yonder, I'll be there...." tells us when the time for all human wants and desires is no more and the day of judgment arrives, when the names in the Book of Life are read, mine will be there.

"Let us lay before the Master from dawn 'till setting sun, let us talk of all his wonderous love and care, then when all of life is over and our work on Earth is done, and the roll is called up yonder I'll be there...." explains that while we live and breathe, we admire, follow and devote our lives to Him for we know because of His grace we will spend eternity with Him.

"When the roll is called up yonder, when the roll is called up yonder, when the roll is called up yonder, when the roll is called up yonder, I'll be there..."says because of my testimony, repentance and my love and acceptance of Jesus Christ as my personal Lord and Savior, my name will be in the Book of Life.

"When the trumpet of the Lord
Shall sound and time shall be no
More"

"And the morning breaks eternal
Bright and fair
When the saved diverse shall
Gather over on the other shore
And the roll is called up yonder,
I'll be there"

"When the roll is called up yonder
When the roll is called up yonder
When the roll is called up
Yonder, I'll be there"

"Let us lay before the Master
From dawn 'till setting sun
Let us talk of all His wonderous
Love and care
Then when all of life is over and
Our work on Earth is done
And the roll is called up yonder,
I'll be there"

"When the roll is called up yonder
When the roll is called up yonder
When the roll is called up yonder
When the roll is called up
Yonder, I'll be there."

> *"Therefore, brethren, stand fast and*
> *hold the traditions which ye have been taught*
> *whether by word or our epistle."*
>   *2* Thessalonians 2:15

REFLECTION PAGE

WHAT IS YOUR FIRST REACTION AFTER LISTENING/READING THIS SONG?

DID THIS SONG INSPIRE YOU TO INCREASE YOUR RELATIONSHIP WITH GOD? WHY?

HOW MUCH DOES MUSIC MINISTRY FIT INTO YOUR WORSHIP?

CHAPTER 31

"THE WAY
(NEW HORIZON)"

Written by: Pat Barrett, Brett Younker,
Karl Martin, Kirby Kaple, Matt Redman

Written by Pat Barrett, Brett Younker, Karl Martin, Kirby Kaple and Matt Redman, "The Way (New Horizon)," was originally released by Housefires as the lead single to their fourth live album, *We Say Yes* (2017).

As Barrett shared in a *Wikipedia* article, the inspiration behind the song, saying, "The way, the truth and the life. It is a simple sentence, but the way it plays out is not always that simple. Over the past couple of years my wife and I had a bunch of changes happen. We just had our 3rd kid recently so we're in the middle of trusting again with more responsibility, pressure and the unknowns in all of it to believe the same thing with more on the line. It can be challenging at times in a real practical sense where your faith plays out. Singing songs that recognize the humanity of faith which is a lot of unknowns and there's something about singing that in a true way without giving fear a platform. We all have our things but its like David said, 'I've set the Lord always before me.'"

In an article by Vince Wright (August 25, 2019), Pat Barrett has been writing and singing music since he was 15 years. He wrote two other popular songs, *Build My Life,* and *Good Father.* Barrett is currently a worship leader at Grace Midtown in Atlanta, Georgia.

"You are the Way (New Horizons)" has become one of the most

popular, motivational and inspirational Christian songs of both young and old Christians played in churches and Christian concerts throughout the world.

"I believe You are the Way, the Truth and the Life...." is a true definition of our Lord and Savior Jesus Christ.

"I believe through every battle, through every heartbreak, through every circumstance, I believe that You are my fortress, You are my portion, You are my hiding place..." tells us having Jesus Christ as personal Lord and Savior is all the protection anyone will ever need.

"I believe through every blessing, through every promise, through every breath I take, I believe that you are provider, You are protector, You are the One I love, yeah..." tells us the realization of everything good in our lives is the result of the love our Lord and Savior has for us.

"It's a new horizon and I'm set on You, And You meet me here today with mercies that are new, all my fears and doubts, they can all come too, because they can't stay long when I'm here with You..." reflects the feeling of being saved and baptized, giving our life and soul to the only One that can give us everything..."

"I believe You are the Way,
The Truth and the Life"

"I believe through every battle
Through every heartbreak
Through every circumstance
I believe that You are my fortress
You are my portion
You are my hiding place"

"I believe You are the Way,
The Truth and the Life"

"I believe through every blessing
Through every promise
Through every breath I take
I believe that You are the provider

You are the protector
You are the One I love, yeah"

"I believe You are the Way
The Truth and the Life"

"It's a new horizon and I'm set on You
And You meet me here today with mercies that are new
All my fears and doubts, they can all come too
Because they can't stay long when I'm here with You"

"I believe You are the Way
The Truth and the Life"

"It's a new horizon and I'm set on You
And you meet me here today with mercies that are new
All my fears and doubts, they can all come too
Because they can't stay long when I'm here with You"

"I believe You are the Way
The Truth and the Life."

*"This is the confidence we have in
approaching God: that if we ask
anything according to His will, He
hears us."*

1 John 5:14 NIV

REFLECTION PAGE

WHAT IS YOUR FIRST REACTION AFTER LISTENING/READING THIS SONG?

DID THIS SONG INSPIRE YOU TO INCREASE YOUR RELATIONSHIP WITH GOD? WHY?

HOW MUCH DOES MUSIC MINISTRY FIT INTO YOUR WORSHIP?

CHAPTER 32

"YOU NEVER LET GO"

Written by: Matt Redman

"You Never Let Go," written by Matt Redman, is a popular and contemporary gospel song full of encouragement and motivation. Redman stated in an interview with *KTIS 98.5* he wrote the song based on the promises in Psalm 23 after his wife had a miscarriage.

The song, which has become a frequent Sunday school favorite among young and old, is the personal prayer of a believer who, amid trials, chooses to trust in God. The lyrics are from direct and indirect Bible verses and is an enthusiastic and exciting way to begin a worship service.

"Even though I walk through the valley of the shadow of death, Your perfect love is casting out fear, and even when I'm caught in the middle of the storms of this life, I won't turn back, I know You are near..." clearly reflects that God is our protector and if He is with us then who can be against us?"

"Oh no, You never let go, through the calm and through the storm, oh no, You never let go, in every high and every low, oh no, You never let go, Lord, You never let go of me..." implies that no matter what trials and tribulations faced, no matter what mistakes may come, knowing He is with us is our peace and salvation.

"And I can see a light that is coming for the heart that holds on, a glorious light beyond all compare, and there will be an end to these troubles, but until that day comes, we'll live to know You here on the earth..." indicates that our faith enables us to know He will be with us, keeping us safe now and throughout eternity.

"And I will fear no evil, for my God is with me, and if my God is with me, whom then shall I fear, whom then shall I fear?..." tells us very bluntly that fear is powerless against us because our love and acceptance of Jesus Christ gives us assured protection forever.

"Even though I walk through the valley of the shadow of death
Your perfect love is casting out fear
And even when I'm caught in the middle of the storms of this life
I won't turn back
I know you are near"

"And I will fear no evil
For my God is with me
And if my God is with me
Whom then shall I fear?
Whom then shall I fear?"

"Oh no, You never let go
Through the calm and through the storm
Oh no, You never let go
In every high and every low
Oh no, you never let go
Lord, You never let go of me"

"And I can see a light that is coming for the heart that holds on
A glorious light beyond all compare
And there will be an end to these troubles
But until that day comes
We'll live to know You here on the earth"

"And I will fear no evil
For my God is with me
And if my God is with me
Whom then shall I fear?
Whom then shall I fear?"

"Oh no, You never let go
Through the calm and through the storm

Oh no, You never let go
In every high and every low
Oh no, You never let go
Lord, You never let go of me"

"Yes I can see a light that is coming for the heart that holds on
And there will be an end to these troubles
But until that day comes
Still I will praise You, still I will praise You"

"Yes I can see a light that is coming for the heart that holds on
And there will be an end to these troubles
But until that day comes
Still I will praise You, still I will praise You"

"Oh no, You never let go
Through the calm and through the storm
Oh no, you never let go
In every high and every low
Oh no, You never let go
Lord, You never let go of me
Oh, You never let go, You never let go"

"Oh no, You never let go
Through the calm and through the storm
Oh no, You never let go
In every high and every low
Oh no, You never let go
Lord You never let go of me
You never let go, You never let go
You never let go of me."

*"Yea though I walk through the
valley of the shadow of death, I
will fear no evil; for thou art with
me; thy rod and thy staff they
comfort me."*

Psalm 23:4

REFLECTION PAGE

WHAT IS YOUR FIRST REACTION AFTER LISTENING/READING THIS SONG?

DID THIS SONG INSPIRE YOU TO INCREASE YOUR RELATIONSHIP WITH GOD? WHY?

HOW MUCH DOES MUSIC MINISTRY FIT INTO YOUR WORSHIP?

CHAPTER 33

"HELLO MY NAME IS"

Written by: Matthew West

"Hello My Name, Is," written by Matthew West, is a popular and highly motivational Christian contemporary song released as his second single from his 2012 album, *Into the Light.* The song was his 5th number one on the *Hot Christian Songs* charts and stayed at that position for seventeen straight weeks.

West wrote a book published in April 2017 which was inspired by the song. In a book interview with *CBN,* West indicated he wrote the book as a sign to "tear off the false name tags that cover up your true identity," and understand who you are as a person.

Most Christian concerts feature the song by one musical group or another and it is also a regular feature of many Sunday morning church services.

"Hello my name is regret, I'm pretty sure we have met, every single day of your life, I'm the whisper inside, that won't let you forget..." reminds us of that which we try to hide deep in our minds, that which we never want to remember, but that which always finds it way to our conscious.

"Hello my name is defeat, I know you recognize me, just when you think you can win, I'll drag you right back down again, till you've lost all belief..." talks of frustration, getting so close and yet still so for away; the desire to succeed but knowing your faith isn't there.

"Hello, my name is the child of the One True King, I've been saved, I've been changed, I have been set free, amazing grace is the song I sing, hello my name is child of the One True King..." is the realization of being saved, a new life, exciting future, and peace of mind, knowing you will spend eternity with our Heavenly Father.

"I am no longer defined, by all the wreckage behind, the One who makes all things new, has proven it's true, just take a look at my life..." gives us the knowledge our past is forgiven and forgotten, a new life begins.

"What love the Father has lavished upon us, that we should be called His children, I am a child of the One True King..." tells us the love of the Father has made us new.

"Hello, my name is regret
I'm pretty sure we have met
Every single day of your life
I'm the whisper inside
That won't let you forget"

"Hello, my name is defeat
I know you recognize me
Just when you think you can win
I'll drag you right back down again
Till you've lost all belief"

"Oh, these are the voices, oh these are the lies
And I have believed them, for the very last time"

"Hello, my name is child of the One True King
I've been saved, I've been changed, I have been set free
Amazing grace is the song I sing
Hello, my name is child of the One True King"

"Woah, woah, woah (woah)
Woah, woah, woah (woah)"

"I am no longer defined
By all the wreckage behind
The One who makes all things new
Has proven it's true
Just take a look at my life"

"Hello my name is child of the One True King
I've been saved, I've been changed, I have been set free
Amazing grace is the song I sing
Hello, my name is child of the One True King"

"Woah, woah, woah (woah)
Woah, woah, woah (woah)
Woah, woah, woah"

"What love the Father has lavished upon us
That we should be called His children
I am a child of the One True King"

"What love the Father has lavished upon us
That we should be called His children
Hello, my name is child of the One True King
I've been saved, I've been changed, I have been set free
Amazing grace is the song I sing
Hello, my name is child of the One True King"

"Woah, woah, woah (woah)
Woah, woah, woah
Woah, woah, woah"

"I am a child of the One True King

"Woah, woah, woah (woah)
Woah, woah, woah (woah)
Woah, woah, woah"

*"Satisfy us in the morning with your
unfailing love, that we may sing for
joy and be glad all our days."*

Psalm 90.14

REFLECTION PAGE

WHAT IS YOUR FIRST REACTION AFTER LISTENING/READING THIS SONG?

DID THIS SONG INSPIRE YOU TO INCREASE YOUR RELATIONSHIP WITH GOD? WHY?

HOW MUCH DOES MUSIC MINISTRY FIT INTO YOUR WORSHIP?

CHAPTER 34

"SPIRIT SING"

Written by Zealand Worship

Zealand Worship is an American-worship band, founded by Phil Joel, from Franklin, Tennessee. Starting to write music in 2015, later releasing *Zealand Worship* and then the extended play (EP) with both Word Records and Warner Records.

"Spirit Sing" is a contemporary Christian song with an inspiring and motivating mood set that is a great feature in any church or Christian music concert.

"You spoke everything into motion, echoing in anything that breathes, Your sound is stirring like the ocean, whispering down deep inside of me..." acknowledges that all existence, the Heavens and the earth, are all created by the Heavenly Father.

"Deep calls out to deep, calls out to deep, calls out to deep..." is illustrative of us when we are in the deepest of our problems, calling out with our most intense and sincere prayers for God's help, love and protection.

"Oh oh oh, You make my spirit sing, oh oh oh, You make my spirit sing out, oh oh oh You're the fire burning in my bones, You're the melody rising in me..." speaks of the driving force of our renewed spirit by God's word.

"You are the finding and the searching, my soul longs for You endlessly, what word can carry this emotion, in this moment I can barely speak..." reflects the overwhelming feeling of love, peace and protection we have for our blessed Savior.

"Oh oh oh
Oh oh oh
You spoke everything into motion
Echoing in anything that breathes
Your sound is stirring like the ocean
Whispering down deep inside of me"

"Deep, calls out to deep
Calls out to deep
Calls out to deep"

"Oh oh oh You make my spirit sing
Oh oh oh You make my spirit sing out
Oh oh oh You're the fire burning in my bones
You're the melody rising in me
Oh oh oh You make my spirit sing"

"You are the finding and the searching
My soul longs for You endlessly
What word can carry this emotion?
In this moment I can barely speak"

"Deep, calls out to deep
Calls out to deep
Calls out to deep"

"Oh oh oh You make my spirit sing
Oh oh oh You make my spirit sing out
Oh oh oh You're the fire burning in my bones
You're the melody rising in me
Oh oh oh You make my spirit sing"

"My heart and lungs cry out in awe of who You are
My heart and lungs cry out to You, the living God
My heart and lungs cry out in awe of who You are
My heart and lungs cry out to You, the living God!"

"You make my spirit sing
(Oh oh oh, oh oh oh)
Oh oh oh You're the fire burning in my bones
You're the melody rising
Oh oh oh
You make my spirit sing
Oh oh oh You make my spirit sing out
(Oh oh oh, oh oh oh)
You make my spirit (sing) sing"

> *"If you love someone, you will be loyal*
> *to him no matter what the cost. You*
> *will always believe in him, always*
> *expect the best of him, and always*
> *stand your ground in defending him."*
>
> 1 Corinthians 13:7 TLB

REFLECTION PAGE

WHAT IS YOUR FIRST REACTION AFTER LISTENING/READING THIS SONG?

DID THIS SONG INSPIRE YOU TO INCREASE YOUR RELATIONSHIP WITH GOD? WHY?

HOW MUCH DOES MUSIC MINISTRY FIT INTO YOUR WORSHIP?

CHAPTER 35

"GRACEFULLY BROKEN"

Written by: Matt Redman, Tasha Cobb Leonard
Zach Williams

"Gracefully Broken," is one of the most emotionally intense and motivating Christian songs of our time and is highly popular in contemporary Christian music circles.

As there are many interpretations of how the Bible describes being gracefully broken, its generally believed that to be gracefully broken is to surrender everything to Him, pouring out our hearts completely, believing that our brokenness has a purpose, and that purpose is that in our brokenness He will make us strong.

God uses brokenness to show that in our weakness, we must rely on His strength. Brokenness is what God uses to replace our self-life with His desires and intentions for us.

"God will break you to position, He will break you to promote you, and break you to put you in your right place, but when He breaks you He doesn't hurt you..." tells us the way we come to Christ, broken with the realization whatever we have tried with our life hasn't worked, won't ever work, and God has let us get to this point to discover where we need to go, to Him.

"Take all I have in these hands, and multiply, God, all that I am, and find my heart on the altar again, set me on fire, set me on fire..." is interpreted to mean take away all I have left in my life, indeed take my life and do with it as you will.

"Here I am God arms wide open, pouring out my life, gracefully broken..." telling God all, totally, completely, unconditionally giving our heart and souls.

"All to Jesus now (yes), all to Jesus now, I'm holding nothing back, holding nothing back..." is the realization that the sacrifice Jesus asks of us is a broken heart and spirit as a broken heart is open to Him and lets in His grace.

"I surrender (I surrender), Y'all throw your hands up and sing I surrender (I surrender)..." is the most powerful part of the song, the unconditional giving of everything we have or will ever have to God.

"Your power at work in me, (Oh) I'm broken gracefully, (Oh) I'm strong when I am weak, (Oh,ooh) I will be free..." is realizing God is taking over our life, with purpose, love and knowing we are someone, a new born child of the King.

"God will break you to position
He will break you to promote you
And break you to put you in your right place
But when He breaks you (Yeah) He doesn't hurt you, He doesn't
When he breaks you He doesn't destroy you, He does it with grace
Anybody been gracefully broken? whoa
Thank you Lord, thank you
So Father tonight, we're broken before You
Thank You for handling us with grace (yeah)
Just lift your worship right there in this moment"

"Take all I have in these hands
And multiply, God, all that I am
And find my heart on the altar again
Set me on fire, set me on fire (c'mon sing)"

"Take all I have in these hands
And multiply, God (God), all that I am
And find my heart on the altar again
Set me on fire (ask him say), set me on fire"

"Here I am, God arms wide open
Pouring out my life
Gracefully broken"

"My heart stands in awe of Your name
Your mighty love stands strong to the end
You will fulfill Your purpose in me
You won't forsake me, You will be with me (You will be with me)"

"Here I am God (say), arms wide open
Pouring out my life
Gracefully broken
Here I am, God arms wide open
Pouring out my life
Gracefully broken"

"All to Jesus now (yes)
All to Jesus now
I'm holding nothing back
Holding nothing back"

"I surrender (I surrender)
Y'all throw your hands up and sing I surrender (I surrender)
Say I surrender (I surrender)
All that I am, I surrender (I surrender)
Have Your way, use me Lord, I surrender, (I surrender)
Do Your will, it's all Your way, I surrender (I surrender)
Use my life for Your glory, say I surrender all (I surrender)
You want to tell Him right where you are (I surrender) let's go"

"Your power at work in me
(Oh) I'm broken gracefully
(Oh) I'm strong when I am weak
(Oh, ooh-oh) I will be free
(Oh, ooh-oh) Your power at work in me
(Oh, ooh-oh) I'm broken gracefully
(Oh, ooh-oh) I'm strong when I am weak
(Oh, ooh-oh) I will be free"

"Your power at work in me
(Oh, ooh-oh) I'm broken gracefully
(Oh, ooh-oh) I'm strong when I am weak
(Oh, ooh-oh) I will be free"

"Your power at work in me
(Oh-ooh-oh) I'm broken gracefully
(Oh-ooh-oh) I'm strong, I'm strong
(Oh-ooh-oh) I will be free yeah"

"For here I am, God arms wide open
Pouring out my life
Gracefully broken"

> *"The heart of man plans his way,*
> *but the Lord establishes his steps."*
>
> Proverbs 16:9

REFLECTION PAGE

WHAT IS YOUR FIRST REACTION AFTER LISTENING/READING THIS SONG?

DID THIS SONG INSPIRE YOU TO INCREASE YOUR RELATIONSHIP WITH GOD? WHY?

HOW MUCH DOES MUSIC MINISTRY FIT INTO YOUR WORSHIP?

CHAPTER 36

"I LOVE TO TELL THE STORY"

Written by: Catherine Hankey
Music by: William G. Fischer

There is no doubt several traditional, well-loved Christian songs have been heard by both Christians and non-Christians who have experienced the same motivation and excitement, one of which is "I Love to Tell the Story."

Written by Catherine Hankey, an English missionary and nurse, who was also known for writing the poem, *The Old, Old Story,* from which two other hymns, *Tell Me the Old Story,* and *I Love to tell the Story* originated.

Hankey became inspired by Methodist John Wesley, began teaching in Sunday schools and was a missionary nurse doing work in the various regions of South Africa. She contracted an illness and spent many months in a hospital bed recuperating. during which time she wrote the poem *Tell Me the Old Old Story of Unseen Things Above.* From this song came the inspiration for "I Love to Tell the Story."

Today, "I Love to Tell the Story," is a favorite of traditional Church services throughout America and is also enjoyed in contemporary services as well.

"I love to tell the story, of unseen things above, of Jesus and His glory, of Jesus and His love...." illustrates the excitement of being saved and the excitement of wanting others to experience the same.

"I love to tell the story, because I know 'tis true, it satisfies my longings, as nothing else can do..." expresses the greatest joy ever, knowing you are one of God's children.

"I love to tell the story, 'twill be my theme in glory, to tell the old, old story, of Jesus and His love..." reflects the pride of knowing you will be known as a man or woman of God.

"I love to tell the story, for some have never heard, the message of salvation, from God's own Holy Word..." defines saving souls by spreading the word as instructed through the Great Commission.

"I love to tell the story, for those who know it best, seem hungering and thirsting, to hear it, like the rest..." lets us remember that even those who know the story are as excited to hear it again as those who hear it for the first time.

"I love to tell the Story,
Of unseen things above
Of Jesus and His glory
of Jesus and His love"

"I love to tell the Story,
Because I know 'Tis True,
It satisfies my longings
As nothing else can do"

"I love to tell the Story,
Twill be my theme in glory
To tell the Old, Old Story
Of Jesus and His love"

"I love to tell the Story,
'Tis pleasant to repeat
What seems, each time I tell it
More wonderfully sweet"

"I love to tell the Story,
For some have never heard
The message of Salvation,
From God's Own Holy Word"

151

"I love to tell the Story,
Twill be my theme in glory,
To tell the Old, Old Story
Of Jesus and His Love"

"I love to tell the Story,
For those who know it best
Seem hungering and thirsting
To hear it, Like the rest."

> *"After this I heard the shouting of a*
> *vast crowd in heaven, 'Hallelujah!'*
> *Praise the Lord! Salvation is from*
> *our God. Honor and authority*
> *belong to Him alone."*
>
> Revelation 19:1 TLB

REFLECTION PAGE

WHAT IS YOUR FIRST REACTION AFTER LISTENING/READING THIS SONG?

DID THIS SONG INSPIRE YOU TO INCREASE YOUR RELATIONSHIP WITH GOD? WHY?

HOW MUCH DOES MUSIC MINISTRY FIT INTO YOUR WORSHIP?

CHAPTER 37

"I BOWED ON MY KNEES AND CRIED HOLY"

Written by: Nettie Dudley Washington
Music by: E.M. Dudley Cantwell

One of the most emotional and intense Christian songs of our time, "I Bowed on My Knees and Cried Holy," was written by Nettie Dudley Washington, with music by E.M. Dudley Cantwell, it appears both in the New National Baptist Hymnal and the African Heritage Hymnal.

In an article by Sharon Baptist Church, Iron Station, NC, describes "I Bowed on My Knees and Cried Holy," as a beautiful, contemporary song that expresses how we will feel when we reach heaven. The song was published in 1977. A popular version of the song is performed regularly by Michael English and Jimmie Davis.

The song tells us how we may feel and what we may experience when we reach heaven. The words tell us of how one would feel first entering heaven, the overwhelming emotion and gratitude for being accepted with everyone we have always loved being there to spend eternity with as well as the desire to meet Jesus.

"...I dreamed of a city called Glory, so bright and so fair, when I entered the gates, I cried, "Holy"...But I said "I want to see Jesus, the One who died for all..." tells us that even when we get to finally see Heaven in all its magnificent beauty, we still long to see the Creator of it all: Jesus.

"...Then I bowed on my knees and cried, Holy, Holy, Holy, I clapped

my hands and sang, 'Glory, Glory to the Son of God..." reflects the
overwhelming emotion, respect, and appreciation for His caring love.

"...As I entered the gates of that city, my loved ones all knew me well,
they took me down the streets of Heaven, such scenes were too many
to tell..." reflects being welcomed by all that we've missed so long and
knowing will never part from again..."

"I dreamed of a city called Glory,
So bright and so fair
When I entered the gates I cried, "Holy"
The angels all met me there:
They carried me from mansion to mansion,
And oh the sights I saw,
But I said, "I want to see Jesus,
The One who died for all"

"Then I bowed on my knees and cried,
"Holy, Holy, Holy"
I clapped my hands and sang, "Glory,
Glory to the Son of God"
I bowed on my knees and cried,
"Holy, Holy, Holy"
Then I clapped my hands and sang, "Glory,
Glory to the Son of God"

"As I entered the gates of that city,
My loved ones all knew me well
They took me down the streets of Heaven
Such scenes were too many to tell,
I saw Abraham, Jacob and Isaac
Talked with Mark and Timothy
But I said, "I want to see Jesus,
'Cause He's the One who died for me"

"Then I bowed on my knees and cried,
Holy, Holy, Holy,
I clapped my hands and sang, 'Glory,
Glory, Glory'
I clapped my hands and sang, 'Glory'
I clapped my hands and sang, 'Glory'
I clapped my hands and sang, 'Glory'
'Glory to the Son of God'
I Sang "Glory to the Son of God."

*"Lord, you have assigned me my
portion and my cup, you have
made my life secure."*

Psalm 16:5 NIV

REFLECTION PAGE

WHAT IS YOUR FIRST REACTION AFTER LISTENING/READING THIS SONG?

DID THIS SONG INSPIRE YOU TO INCREASE YOUR RELATIONSHIP WITH GOD? WHY?

HOW MUCH DOES MUSIC MINISTRY FIT INTO YOUR WORSHIP?

"CAN THE CIRCLE BE UNBROKEN?"

Originally Written by: Ada R. Habershon
Music by: Charles H. Gabriel
Re-Written by: A.P. Carter

Originally written as "Will the Circle be Unbroken?", in 1907, by Ada R. Habershon, and music composed by Charles H. Gabriel, today the song's more familiar version was re-written by A.P. Carter with most performances credited to the Carter Family, entitled "Can the Circle be Unbroken?"

The Carter version does use basically the same music but with some change in verse structure and lyrics. As reported in *Genius: Song Lyrics Finder,* the song was initially written as a funeral song, and asks the question many of us wonder about today, "how does death interrupt the circle of family life, if at all?"

"Can the Circle be Unbroken?", also asks the question, "will our families be re-united in heaven, are we prepared and will we spend eternity together or will the family circle we enjoy on earth not be as inclusive?"

"Can the Circle be Unbroken?", does give the idea that hope for a blessed reunion in heaven one day with all of us together is possible and that we indeed will see each again.

"I was standing by the window, on one cold and cloudy day, and saw the hearse coming for to carry my mother away..." allows us to know that even with the hardest, most painful of times, we know our faith will be sufficient to carry us through.

"Can the circle be unbroken, by and by Lord, by and by..." asks the question, can our human circle of life here on earth, once severed, be sewn together again one day?"

"Oh, I followed close behind her, tried to hold up and be brave, but I could not hide my sorrow, when they laid her in the grave..." reminds us that although letting some loved one leave us is painful and sorrowful, our faith is the guarantee from our Blessed Savior that it will only be temporary.

"I went back home, Lord, my home was lonesome, since my mother, she was gone..." illustrates the emotion coming with the realization that our loved one is no longer with us but also ignites the determination to assure our life is heading in the direction to one day meet again.

"I was standing by the window
On one cold and cloudy day
And I saw the hearse come rolling
For to carry my mother away"

"Can the circle be unbroken
By and by Lord, by and by
There's a better home awaiting
In the sky, Lord, in the sky"

"Lord, I told the undertaker,
Undertaker please drive slow
For this body you are hauling
Lord, I hate to see her go"

"Can the circle be unbroken
By and by Lord, by and by
There's a better home awaiting
In the sky, Lord in the sky"

"Oh, I followed close behind her
Tried to hold up and be brave
But I could not hide my sorrow
When they laid her in the grave"

"Can the circle be unbroken
By and by Lord, by and by
There's a better home awaiting
In the sky, Lord, in the sky"

"I went back home, Lord, my home was lonesome
Since my mother, she was gone
All my brothers and sisters crying
What a home so sad and alone"

"Can the circle be unbroken
By and by Lord, by and by
There's a better home awaiting
In the sky, Lord, in the sky."

*"Therefore, since we are surrounded
by such a great cloud of witnesses, let
us throw off everything that hinders
and the sin that so easily entangles,
and let us run with perseverance the
race marked out for us. Let us fix our
eyes on Jesus."*

Hebrews 12:1-2 NIV

REFLECTION PAGE

WHAT IS YOUR FIRST REACTION AFTER LISTENING/READING THIS SONG?

DID THIS SONG INSPIRE YOU TO INCREASE YOUR RELATIONSHIP WITH GOD? WHY?

HOW MUCH DOES MUSIC MINISTRY FIT INTO YOUR WORSHIP?

CHAPTER 39

"GIVE ME THAT OLD-TIME RELIGION"

Written by: G.D. Pike
Re-Written by: Charles Davis Tillman

One of the most recognized of traditional gospel music, "Give Me that Old-Time Religion," continues to motivate church congregations with easy to remember lyrics and inspirational meaning.

First published in 1873, by G.D. Pike, it was again published in 1891, by Charles Davis Tillman. It has since become a traditional favorite in many Protestant hymnals, though it says nothing about Jesus or the gospel.

The song was initially a song popular in African-American circles but after Tillman re-wrote the song and published it again in 1891, it began to have influence in black spiritual and white gospel music forming what is now referred to as southern gospel.

"Give me that old-time religion, give me that old-time religion...it's good enough for me..." refers to the Word, the Bible, Ten Commandments and what life was, is, and will always be, the story of faith.

"It was good for our mothers...it was good for our mothers and it's good enough for me..." reflects the love and faith of our mothers is a model for our lives.

"Makes me love everybody...and it's good enough for me..." acknowledges a faith that is wrapped in love is a gift for all of us.

"It will take us all to heaven...and it's good enough for me..." tells us our faith and love in Jesus Christ will give us eternal salvation in heaven.

"Give me that old-time religion
Give me that old-time religion
Give me that old-time religion
It's good enough for me"

"Give me that old-time religion
Give me that old-time religion
Give me that old-time religion
It's good enough for me"

"It was good for our mothers
It was good for our mothers
It was good for our mothers
And it's good enough for me"

"Give me that old-time religion
Give me that old-time religion
Give me that old-time religion
It's good enough for me"

"Makes me love everybody
Makes me love everybody
Makes me love everybody
And it's good enough for me"

"Give me that old-time religion
Give me that old-time religion
Give me that old-time religion
It's good enough for me"

"It will take us all to heaven
It will take us all to heaven
It will take us all to heaven
And it's good enough for me"

MICHAEL E. PAYTON, MA

"Give me that old-time religion
Give me that old-time religion
Give me that old-time religion
It's good enough for me"

"One more time"

"Give me that old-time religion
Give me that old-time religion
Give me that old-time religion
It's good enough for me (for me)"

> *"The mind controlled by the Spirit is*
> *life and peace."*
>
> Romans 8:6 NIV

REFLECTION PAGE

WHAT IS YOUR FIRST REACTION AFTER LISTENING/READING THIS SONG?

DID THIS SONG INSPIRE YOU TO INCREASE YOUR RELATIONSHIP WITH GOD? WHY?

HOW MUCH DOES MUSIC MINISTRY FIT INTO YOUR WORSHIP?

CHAPTER 40

"PUT YOUR HAND
IN THE HAND"

Written by: Gene MacLellan

One of the more inspirational, gospel songs of the last century has been "Put Your Hand in the Hand," written by Gene MacLellan and initially recorded by Anne Murray.

Later the song became a hit for the Canadian band, *Ocean,* and peaked at No. 2, on the U.S. *Billboard Hot 100,* and remained in the top 10 for seven weeks, being finally ranked as the No. 33 song for 1971, according to *Billboard.*

As reported in an article of *Country Thang Daily,* "Put Your Hand in the Hand," talks about establishing an essential relationship with God, having faith, and trusting the Lord with all your heart. The song is very straightforward in telling us to trust the Lord and have faith in Him. The song is primarily a reminder not to lose faith as we continue to live the life we have.

"Put your hand in the hand of the man who stilled the water...put your hand in the hand of the man from Galilee..." very clearly, the message is follow the One who deserves to be followed.

"My momma taught me to pray before I reached the age of seven..." tells us a solid foundation to raise children include knowing God early in life, helps in the appreciation of Him throughout life.

"Put your hand in the hand of the man who stilled the water, put your hand in the hand of the man who calmed the sea, take a look at yourself and you can look at others differently..." is the realization that once saved we do see a new person in the mirror of life, fresh with love, caring and with respect for self and others.

"Put your hand in the hand of the man
Who stilled the water
Put your hand in the hand of the man
Who calmed the sea
Take a look at yourself
And you can look at others differently
Put your hand in the hand of the man
from Galilee"

"My momma taught me how to pray
Before I reached the age of seven
When I'm down on my knees
That's when I'm closest to heaven
Daddy lived his life, two kids and a wife
Well you do what you must do
But he showed me enough
Of what it takes
To get me through, oh yeh!"

"Put your hand in the hand of the man
Who stilled the water
Put your hand in the hand of the man
Who calmed the sea
Take a look at yourself
And you can look at others differently
Put your hand in the hand of the man
From Galilee
Oh yeh!"

"Put your hand in the hand of the man
Who stilled the water
Put your hand in the hand of the man
Who calmed the sea
Take a look at yourself
And you can look at others differently
Put your hand in the hand of the man
From Galilee
Oh yeh!"

"Put your hand in the hand of the man
Who stilled the water
Put your hand in the hand of the man
Who calmed the sea
Take a look at yourself
And You can look at others differently
Put your hand in the hand of the man
From Galilee
Oh Yeh!
Put your hand in the hand of the man from Galilee
Put your hand in the hand of the man from Galilee, Oh yeh!"

> *"If you love someone, you will be loyal*
> *to him no matter what the cost. You*
> *will always believe in him, always*
> *expect the best of him, and always*
> *stand your ground in defending him.*
> 1 Corinthians 13:7 TLB

REFLECTION PAGE

WHAT IS YOUR FIRST REACTION AFTER LISTENING/READING THIS SONG?

DID THIS SONG INSPIRE YOU TO INCREASE YOUR RELATIONSHIP WITH GOD? WHY?

HOW MUCH DOES MUSIC MINISTRY FIT INTO YOUR WORSHIP?

CHAPTER 41

"MY JESUS"

Written by: Anne Wilson
Jeff Pardo, Matthew West

As reported in an article by *Waynation,* Anne Wilson and her family experienced a devastating tragedy. A hopeless situation forced Anne to evaluate who God really is. She had to decide if she believed God and if she could trust Him even when it didn't make sense. Through processing this life event and learning to worship through hardship, God led Anne on a different journey than she expected. He is giving her the opportunity to share her story and to give hope and encouragement to others who are in difficult times.

This experience also inspired "My Jesus." The song is a worshipful tribute to her Heavenly Father that demonstrates her desire for people to know that Jesus can help us through any situation we are going through. It also reminds us that God uses our trials, so we can help others and tell our story of how God works in our lives.

A beautiful and inspiring song, "My Jesus," tells a great story and a very moving and emotional testimony to our blessed Lord and Savior Jesus Christ.

"Are you past the point of weary...let me tell you 'bout Jesus..." lets us know that no matter how hopeless and helpless you may believe you are, there will always be One who is there for you.

"Do you feel that empty feeling...let me tell you 'bout Jesus..." says no matter what we've done, no matter how bad, there's always an answer: Jesus.

"He makes a way where there ain't no way...let me tell you 'bout Jesus..." tells us nothing is impossible with Jesus.

"We can wipe away the tears, from broken dreams and wasted years... let me tell you 'bout Jesus..." references us that only God can remove the past, the bad, the sin, the hurt, the pain and the guilt and renew your life.

"And the good news is I know that He can do for you what He's done for me...let me tell you 'bout Jesus..." expresses the excitement to get others to find Jesus.

"Who would take my cross to Calvary, pay the price for all my guilty... let me tell you 'bout Jesus..." speaks of the greatest example of His love.

"Are you past the point of weary?
Is your burden weighing heavy?
Is it all too much to carry?
Let me tell you "bout my Jesus"

"Do you feel that empty feeling?
"Cause shame's done all its stealing
And you're desperate for some healing
Let me tell you 'bout my Jesus"

"He makes a way where there ain't no way
Rises up from an empty grave
Ain't no sinner that He can't save
Let me tell you 'bout my Jesus"

"His love is strong and His grace is free
And the good news is I know that He
Can do for you what He's done for me
Let me tell you 'bout my Jesus
And let my Jesus change your life"

"Hallelujah, hallelujah
Hallelujah, amen, amen"

"Who can wipe away the tears
From broken dreams and wasted years
And tell the past to disappear? Oh
Let me tell you 'bout my Jesus"

"And all the wrong turns that you would
Go and undo if you could
Who can work it all for your good
Let me tell you 'bout my Jesus"

"He makes a way where there ain't no way
Rises up from an empty grave
Ain't no sinner that He can't save
Let me tell you 'bout my Jesus"

"His love is strong and His grace is free
And the good news is I know that He
Can do for you what He's done for me
Let me tell you 'bout my Jesus
And let my Jesus change your life"

"Hallelujah, hallelujah
Hallelujah, amen, amen,
Amen"

"Who would take my cross to Calvary?
Pay the price for all my guilty?
Who would care that much about me?
Let me tell you 'bout my Jesus, oh"

"He makes a way where there ain't no way
Rises up from an empty grave
Ain't no sinner that He can't save
Let me tell you 'bout my Jesus"

"His love is strong and His grace is free
And the good news is I know that He

Can do for you what He's done for me
Let me tell you 'bout my Jesus
And let my Jesus change your life"

"Hallelujah, hallelujah
Hallelujah, amen, amen
Hallelujah, hallelujah
Hallelujah (amen, amen)
Let my Jesus change your life"

> *"Listen, my son, accept what I say, and
> the years of your life will be many. I
> guide you in the way of wisdom and
> lead you along straight paths."*
> Proverbs 4:10-11 NIV

REFLECTION PAGE

WHAT IS YOUR FIRST REACTION AFTER LISTENING/READING THIS SONG?

DID THIS SONG INSPIRE YOU TO INCREASE YOUR RELATIONSHIP WITH GOD? WHY?

HOW MUCH DOES MUSIC MINISTRY FIT INTO YOUR WORSHIP?

CHAPTER 42

"HEALER"

Written by: Kari Jobe

"Healer," is a contemporary Christian song, written by Kari Jobe. Jobe has received two *Grammy Award* nominations and ten *Dove Award nominations*, winning six, for her first album in 2009.

As reported in the article, "The Story Behind the Song," in *Christian Contemporary Music and Going Deeper.*

"Healer," is a song about God being our Healer. The lyrics are like a declaration to Him saying that we trust that He will heal us from anything whether it may be a sickness, a sin, a struggle, or a hindrance. It also reinforces on what God does: He walks us through every moment and knows our deepest need.

The song is performed in many Christian concerts throughout the country and also in church services and is a favorite on Christian radio stations across the country.

"You hold my every moment, You calm my raging seas, You walk me through the fire..." acknowledges that we have given Him our life and He now is our life.

"I believe You're my healer, I believe You are all I need, I believe..." demonstrates the full faith, love and loyalty to our Savior.

"And I believe You're my portion, I believe You're more than enough for me..." is our realization that the only part of our life that we really need is God's part for without it the rest of our life is pointless.

"Nothing is impossible for You…You hold my world in Your hands.." implies that God is all powerful with no limitations.

"Lord I believe You're more than enough for me, Jesus You're all I need…" is testimony to God that our lives revolve around Him.

"You hold my every moment
You calm my raging seas
You walk with me through fire
And heal all my disease
I trust in You, I trust in You"

"I believe You're my healer
I believe You are all I need
I believe"

"And I believe You're my portion
I believe You're more than enough for me
Jesus You're all I need"

"You hold my every moment
You calm my raging seas
You walk with me through fire
And heal all my disease
I trust in You, Lord I trust in You"

"I believe You're my healer
I believe You are all I need
Oh, I believe"

"I believe You're my portion
I believe You're more than enough for me
Jesus, You're all I need"

"Nothing is impossible for You
Nothing is impossible
Nothing is impossible for You
You hold my world in Your hands"

"Nothing is impossible for You
Nothing is impossible
Nothing is impossible for You
You hold my world in Your hands"

"I believe You're my healer
I believe You are all I need
Oh, yes You are, Yes You are"

"And I believe You're my portion
Lord I believe You're more than enough for me
Jesus You're all I need
More than enough for me
Jesus You are all I need"

"You're my healer!"

*"Blessings on all who reverence and
Trust the Lord-on all who obey him!
Their reward shall be prosperity and
Happiness.*

Psalm 128:1-2 TLB

REFLECTION PAGE

WHAT IS YOUR FIRST REACTION AFTER LISTENING/READING THIS SONG?

DID THIS SONG INSPIRE YOU TO INCREASE YOUR RELATIONSHIP WITH GOD? WHY?

HOW MUCH DOES MUSIC MINISTRY FIT INTO YOUR WORSHIP?

CHAPTER 43

"ANGELS AMONG US"

Written by: Don Goodman
Becky Hobbs
Recorded by: Alabama

One of the most moving and beautiful contemporary Christian songs in recent years, it is written by Don Goodman and Becky Hobbs.

In an article published by *Country Thang Daily,* Hobbs said the song was written based on premonitions which Hobbs believed were sent to her protecting her and her band members from perishing in a tragic vehicle accident in 1986. Hobbs believed the voice of the premonitions was her guardian angel and she spent the next few years writing the lyrics and then asked Don Goodman to help her finish the song.

"Angels Among Us," was recorded by Alabama, and released in December 1993, as a Christmas single from the band's 1993 album, *Cheap Seats.*

"I was walkin' home from school on a cold winter day, took a shortcut through the woods, and I lost my way...but then a kind old man took my hand and led me home..." illustrates those who believe will indeed be protected by Him who loves us.

"Oh, I believe there are angels among us...to show us how to live, to teach us how to give, to guide us with the light above..." tells us He acts when He feels it's right, not when we do, but He is always there.

"Oh I believe there are angels among us...they come to us in our darkest hours..." says He is always looking after us who believe, in the bad times He is always there, as He is in the good times.

"I was walkin" home from school on a cold winter day
Took a shortcut through the woods, and I lost my way
It was getting' late, and I was scared and alone
But then a kind old man took my hand and led me home
Mama couldn't see him, but he was standin' there
And I knew in my heart, he was the answer to my prayers"

"Oh I believe there are angels among us
Sent down to us from somewhere up above
They come to you and me in our darkest hours
To show us how to live, to teach us how to give
To guide us with the light of love"

"When life held troubled times, and had me down on my knees
There's always been someone there to come along and comfort me
A kind word from a stranger, to lend a helpin' hand
A phone call from a friend, just to say I understand
And ain't it kind of funny that at the dark end of the road
Someone lights the way with just a single ray of hope"

"Oh I believe there are angels among us
Sent down to us from somewhere up above
They come to you and me in our darkest hours
To show us how to live, to teach us how to give"

"To guide us with the light of love
They wear so many faces; show up in the strangest places
To grace us with their mercy, in our time of need"

"Oh I believe there are angels among us
Sent down to us from somewhere up above
They come to you and me in our darkest hours
To show us how to live, to teach us how to give
To guide us with the light of love
To guide us with the light of love."

"If you have any encouragement from
Being united with Christ, if any
Comfort from His love, if any
Fellowship with the Spirit, if any
Tenderness and compassion, then
Make my joy complete by being
Like-minded, having the same love,
Being one in spirit and purpose."

Philippians 2:1-2 NIV

REFLECTION PAGE

WHAT IS YOUR FIRST REACTION AFTER LISTENING/READING THIS SONG?

DID THIS SONG INSPIRE YOU TO INCREASE YOUR RELATIONSHIP WITH GOD? WHY?

HOW MUCH DOES MUSIC MINISTRY FIT INTO YOUR WORSHIP?

CHAPTER 44

"GLORIOUS GOD"

Written by: Lauren Talley

Absolutely Gospel Music, in January 2020, published an article related to Lauren Talley and her current single at the time, "Glorious God."

The song shares the creation story and recognizes all God created to give us the lives we live. The song is a reminder that God's presence is all around, everywhere we are.

Talley is one of Christian music's most dynamic talents and has inspired a generation of young people to serve the Lord. She has recorded five solo albums, her most recent being the 2017 release, *"The Gospel,"* which she produced, wrote, and sang.

"You poured out the water, raised up a mountain, imagined the heavens, I can't even fathom how good You are, how good You are..." indicates the amazement we have for the awesome, unlimited power of our God.

"Glorious glorious God, wonderful Maker, I'll sing with the stars and praise my Creator...." is the praise and gratitude for the One we owe all too.

"...with one single motion You wrote every bird song, composed my emotions..." reflects His control of the elements, the creatures of the Earth and the emotions of our lives.

"You poured out the water
Raised up a mountain
Imagined the heavens
I can't even fathom how good You are how good You are

With one single motion You wrote ev'ry bird song
Composed my emotions
I can't even fathom how good You are how good You are"

"Glorious glorious God, wonderful Maker
I'll sing with the stars and praise my Creator
O glorious glorious God
O glorious glorious God"

"You poured out the water
Raised up a mountain
Imagined the heavens
I can't even fathom how good You are how good You are
With one single motion You wrote ev'ry bird song
Composed my emotions
I can't even fathom how good You are how good You are"

"Glorious glorious God wonderful Maker
I'll sing with the stars and praise my Creator
O glorious glorious God
O glorious glorious God"

"And it was good for God is good
And it was good Lord You are good"

"Glorious glorioous God wonderful Maker
I'll sing with the stars and praise my Creator
O glorious glorious God
O glorious glorious God"

*"Moreover, because of what Christ has
done, we have become gifts to God
that He delights in, for as part of
God's sovereign plan we were chosen
from the beginning to be His, and all
things happen just as He decided long ago."*
Ephesians 1:11 TLB

REFLECTION PAGE

WHAT IS YOUR FIRST REACTION AFTER LISTENING/READING THIS SONG?

DID THIS SONG INSPIRE YOU TO INCREASE YOUR RELATIONSHIP WITH GOD? WHY?

HOW MUCH DOES MUSIC MINISTRY FIT INTO YOUR WORSHIP?

CHAPTER 45

"HOUSE OF THE LORD"

Written by: Phil Wickham

"House of the Lord," written by Phil Wickman, peaked at number one on the US *Hot Christian Songs* chart. The song also made it to number 12 on the *Bubbling Under Hot 100* chart. "House of the Lord," also received two *GMA Dove Award nominations* for Song of the Year and Pop/Contemporary Recorded Song of the Year at the *2022 GMA Dove Awards*.

Wickham released "House of the Lord," in April 2021, as the second single from his album *Hymn of Heaven*. In a story reported in *Wikipedia*, he shared, "Over the past 12 months I've learned in a deeper way than ever that though happiness comes and goes in Jesus I can always have joy. Because though happiness is based on circumstances, joy is rooted in identity. It's based on who God says we are...though we were once beggars, in Jesus we are royalty."

The contemporary Christian hit "House of the Lord," has fast become a favorite of old and young alike and motivates enthusiasm and praise on Christian radio, at revivals, concerts and church services.

"We worship the God who was, we worship the God who is, we worship the God who evermore will be..." is testimony about the awesome power and splendor of our Heavenly Father.

"There's joy in the house of the Lord, there's Joy in the house of the Lord today..." is acknowledgment that happiness, joy and love are rewards of the eternal life we will have by accepting Christ as our personal Lord and Savior.

"We sing to the God who heals, we sing to the God who saves, we sing to the God who always makes a way..." expresses our thanks for His love and compassion in our lives.

"We were the beggars, now we're royalty, we were prisoners, now we're running free..." tells of His forgiveness for our sins, crimes and disregard for others.

"We shout out Your praise, there's joy in the house today, we shout out Your praise..." is open, uninhibited praise and gratitude for our Savior and all He has done for us.

"We worship the God who was
We worship the God who is
We worship the God who evermore will be
He opened the prison doors
He parted the raging sea
My God
He holds the victory"

"There's joy
In the house of the Lord
There's joy in the house of the Lord today
And we won't be quiet
We shout out
Your praise
There's joy in the house of the Lord
Our God is surely in this place
And we won't be quiet
We shout out Your praise"

"We shout out Your praise"

"We sing to the God who heals
We sing to the God who saves
We sing to the God who always makes a way
He hung upon that cross
Then He rose up from that grave
My God's still rolling stones away"

MICHAEL E. PAYTON, MA

"There's joy in the house of the Lord
There's joy in the House of the Lord today
And we won't be quiet
We shout out Your praise
There's joy in the house of the Lord
Our God is surely in this place
And we won't be quiet
We shout out Your praise"

"We were the beggars
Now we're royalty
We were the prisoners
Now we're running free
We are forgiven, accepted
Redeemed by His grace"

"Let the house of the Lord sing praise"

"Cause we were the beggars
Now we're royalty
We were the prisoners
Now we're running free
We are forgiven, accepted
Redeemed by His grace
Let the house of the Lord sing praise"

"There's joy
In the house of the Lord
There's joy in the house of the Lord today
And we won't be quiet
We shout out Your praise
There's joy in the house of the Lord
Our God is surely in this place
And we won't be quiet
We shout out Your praise"

"There's joy in the house of the Lord
There's joy in the house of the Lord today
And we won't be quiet
We shout out Your praise
There's joy in the house of the Lord
Our God is surely in this place
And we won't be quiet
We shout out Your praise"

"We shout out Your praise
There's joy in the house today
We shout out Your praise
We shout out Your praise"

*"You will keep in perfect peace, Him
whose mind is steadfast because He
trusts in you. Trust in the Lord,
forever, for the Lord, the Lord, is the
Rock eternal.*

Isaiah 26:3 NIV

REFLECTION PAGE

WHAT IS YOUR FIRST REACTION AFTER LISTENING/READING THIS SONG?

DID THIS SONG INSPIRE YOU TO INCREASE YOUR RELATIONSHIP WITH GOD? WHY?

HOW MUCH DOES MUSIC MINISTRY FIT INTO YOUR WORSHIP?

"FAMILY BIBLE"

Written by: Willie Nelson

"Family Bible," is a country gospel song, written by country singer Willie Nelson. According to information reported on *Wikipedia,* Nelson began writing the song in 1957. After assuming financial issues, he sold the song to Paul Buskirk, who then took it to Claude Gray whose recording of the song reached number seven on *Billboard Hot Country Singles.*

Eventually Nelson, who moved into Nashville by this time, had been receiving recognition for writing the song and he made it part of his live performance set, and he recorded it for the first time himself in his 1971 album *Yesterday's Wine.*

Willie Nelson's inspiration for "Family Bible," came from his grandmother, Nancy Elizabeth Smothers, who would sing *Rock of Ages,* and read from the Bible after each supper. The song brings back memories to many of the same scenario they experienced growing up: the family sitting together eating supper every evening and then someone reading a verse from the family Bible, the most treasured item in the house. The family Bible was where all important family documents, i.e., birth certificates, death certificates, bank account information, house titles, etc., were stored within the front or back covers.

"There's a family Bible on the table, each page is torn and hard to read..." illustrates the importance of faith to the family structure.

"Dad would read to us from the family Bible, and we'd count our many blessings one by one..." causes a resemblance of precious memories resulting from families with their priorities solid and needing no interpretation,

"...I can see us sittin' round the table, when from the family Bible dad would read, I can hear my mother softly singing..." symbolic of worshiping as a family circle.

"There's a family Bible on the table
Each page is torn and hard to read
But the family Bible on the table
Will ever be my key to memories
At the end of day when work was over
And when the evening meal was done"

"Dad would read to us from the family Bible
And we'd count our many blessings one by one
I can see us sittin' round the table
When from the family Bible dad would read
I can hear my mother softly singing
Rock of ages rock of ages cleft for me"

"Now this old world of ours is full of trouble
This old world would also better be
If we'd find more Bibles on the tables
And mother's singing Rock of Ages cleft for me
I can see us sittin' round the table
When from the family Bible Dad would read
I can hear my mother softly singing
Rock of ages rock of ages cleft for me
Rock of ages rock of ages cleft for me"

"Trust and reverence the Lord....then
you will be given renewed health and vitality."
Proverbs 3: 7-8 TLB

REFLECTION PAGE

WHAT IS YOUR FIRST REACTION AFTER LISTENING/READING THIS SONG?

DID THIS SONG INSPIRE YOU TO INCREASE YOUR RELATIONSHIP WITH GOD? WHY?

HOW MUCH DOES MUSIC MINISTRY FIT INTO YOUR WORSHIP?

CHAPTER 47

"VICTORY IN JESUS"

Eugene Monroe Bartlett, Sr.

Eugene Bartlett Sr., born in 1885, in Waynesville, Missouri, attended Hall-Moody Institute in Tennessee and William Jewell College in Missouri. In 1921 he established the Hartford Music Company, which became one of the first publishing companies for Southern Gospel music. In 1973, he was inducted into the Gospel Music Association Hall of Fame in Nashville, Tennessee.

As reported in an article by Diana Leagh Matthews, *"Rebel to Redeemed...Sharing His Kind of Love,"* Bartlett wrote over more than 800 songs. After suffering a stroke that left him partially paralyzed, he did continue to study his Bible, looking forward to the eternal victory he knew was approaching.

It was during the time after the stroke he wrote the words to "Victory in Jesus." First appearing in a songbook paperback, "Gospel Choruses," it was the final song Bartlett wrote. The song became his best known and well-loved work. The song is an optimistic reminder of the hope of heaven.

"I heard an old, old story, how a Savior came from glory, how He gave His life on Calvary..." talks of God sending His only Son to die for our opportunity to spend eternity with Him.

"O victory in Jesus, my Savior forever, He sought me, He bought me, with His redeeming blood..." lets us understand the He died for us even though we didn't know Him, just so we could meet Him.

"I heard about His healing, of His cleansing pow'r revealing, how He made the lame to walk again, and cause the blind to see..." refers to the miracles and amazing guidance He gives us all for a price we can all pay: giving our hearts, souls and lives to Him.

"And I heard about the streets of gold, beyond the crystal sea, about the Angels singing..." is the beautiful picture we of faith have in what our reward will be one day.

"I heard an old, old story,
How a Savior came from glory,
How He gave His life on Calvary
To save a wretch like me;
I heard about His groaning,
Of His precious blood's atoning
Then I repented of my sins
And won the victory"

"O victory in Jesus,
My Savior, forever;
He sought me and bought me
With His redeeming blood;
He loved me ere I knew Him
And all my love is due Him,
He plunged me to victory,
Beneath the cleansing flood"

"I heard about His healing,
Of His cleansing pow'r revealing
How He made the lame to walk again
And caused the blind to see;
And then I cried, "Dear Jesus,
Come and heal my broken spirit,"
And somehow Jesus came and bro't
To me the victory"

"O victory in Jesus,
My Savior, forever
He sought me and bought me
With His redeeming blood;
He loved me ere I knew Him
And all my love is due Him,
He plunged me to victory,
Beneath the cleansing flood"

"I heard about a mansion
He has built for me in glory
And I heard about the streets of gold
Beyond the crystal sea;
About the angels singing,
And the old redemption story,
And some sweet day I'll sing up there
The song of victory"

"O victory in Jesus
My Savior, forever
He sought me and bought me
With His redeeming blood;
He loved me ere I knew Him
And all my love is due Him
He plunged me to victory
Beneath the cleansing flood."

"We are pressed on every side by
troubles, but not crushed and broken.
We are perplexed because we don't
know why things happen as they do,
but we don't give up and quit. We are
hunted down, but God never
abandons us.
2 Corinthians 4:8-9 TLB

REFLECTION PAGE

WHAT IS YOUR FIRST REACTION AFTER LISTENING/READING THIS SONG?

DID THIS SONG INSPIRE YOU TO INCREASE YOUR RELATIONSHIP WITH GOD? WHY?

HOW MUCH DOES MUSIC MINISTRY FIT INTO YOUR WORSHIP?

CHAPTER 48

"NOTHING BUT THE BLOOD"

Written by: Robert Lowry

"Nothing But the Blood," is a well-known and traditional Christian hymn about the blood atonement and propitiation for sin by the death of Jesus as explained in Hebrews 9, written by Robert Lowry, a Baptist minister and a professor at Bucknell University.

Lowry wrote the song in 1876 and it debuted at a camp meeting in Ocean Grove, New Jersey. In recent years, the song has been performed, not just in traditional church services but in contemporary churches as well. *Discipleship Ministries* reports that the Rev. Carlton R. Young, editor of *The United Methodist Hymnal* noted that "Nothing but the Blood," was one of the top popular religious songs used in five widely used hymnals and songbooks.

In recent years "Nothing But the Blood" has been performed at concerts throughout the world by such entertainers and Carrie Underwood and Randy Travis and continues to be accepted and enjoyed by Christians of all ages.

"What can wash away my sin, nothing but the blood of Jesus..." tells us our sins have all been forgiven and forgotten by the blood of the Sacrifice of Christ.

"Oh precious is the flow, that makes me white as snow..." says the blood pouring from His body washed away the dirt of sin and made our souls pure.

"For my pardon, this I see, nothing but the blood of Jesus..." reminds us His blood opened the door to our Salvation.

"This is all my hope and peace...this is all my righteousness..." explains that hope for our salvation is only possible through Christ's blood.

"What can wash away my sin?
Nothing but the blood of Jesus"

"What can make me whole again?
Nothing but the blood of Jesus"

"Oh! precious is the flow
That makes me white as snow
No other fount I know
Nothing but the blood of Jesus"

"For my pardon, this I see
Nothing but the blood of Jesus"

"For my cleansing this my plea,
Nothing but the blood of Jesus
Nothing can for sin atone,
Nothing but the blood of Jesus
Naught of good that I have done
Nothing but the blood of Jesus"

"This is all my hope and peace,
Nothing but the blood of Jesus
This is all my righteousness,
Nothing but the blood of Jesus"

*"How much more shall the blood
of Christ, who through the eternal
Spirit offered himself without spot
to God, purge your conscience
from dead works to serve the living God."*

Hebrews 9:14

REFLECTION PAGE

WHAT IS YOUR FIRST REACTION AFTER LISTENING/READING THIS SONG?

DID THIS SONG INSPIRE YOU TO INCREASE YOUR RELATIONSHIP WITH GOD? WHY?

HOW MUCH DOES MUSIC MINISTRY FIT INTO YOUR WORSHIP?

"I WILL SING OF MY REDEEMER"

Written by: Philip Bliss
Music by: James McGranahan

Enjoying the Journey," presented an article on Philip Bliss, who wrote the hymn, "I Will Sing of My Redeemer," which became the first hymn to be recorded on the phonograph, which was recorded by George C. Stebbins. The song also, is considered the last song Bliss wrote before his tragic death in a train accident.

"I Will Sing of My Redeemer," is a hymn praising our Savior for laying down His life on Calvary. The song was discovered in the wreckage of a train wreck where he and his wife perished in December 29, 1876. James McGranahan later composed the music.

Other hymns written by Bliss included *Almost Persuaded, Dare to be a Daniel, Hallelujah "Tis Done!, Hallenlujah What a Savior,* and *Let the Lower Lights Be Burning.* "I Will Sing of My Redeemer," is a great, traditional Christian hymn standing today as a respected and moving tribute to our beloved Savior.

"I will sing of my Redeemer, and His wonderous love to me...on the cruel cross He suffered, from the curse He set me free..." reflects gratitude for the sacrifice and praise of His love for us.

"Sing, Oh sing of my Redeemer, with His blood, He purchased me, on the cross, He sealed my pardon, paid the debt, and made me free..." tells us His death and blood opened the door for our salvation.

"I will tell the wondrous story, how my lost estate, to save in His boundless love and mercy, He, the ransom freely gave..." acknowledges He gave His blood to wash away our sins and give us eternal salvation.

"I will sing of my Redeemer
And His wondrous love to me;
On the cruel cross He suffered
From the curse He set me free"

"Sing, Oh sing of my Redeemer
With His blood, He purchased me,
On the cross, He sealed my pardon,
Paid the debt, And made me free"

"I will tell the wondrous story
How my lost estate, To save.
In His boundless love and mercy,
He, The ransom freely gave."

"Sing, Oh sing of my Redeemer
With His blood, He purchased me,
On the cross, He sealed my pardon,
Paid the debt, And made me free"

"I will praise my dear Redeemer,
His triumphant pow'r I'll tell,
How the victory He giveth
Over sin, And death, And hell."

"Sing, Oh sing of my Redeemer
With His blood, He purchased me
On the cross, He sealed my pardon,
Paid the debt, And made me free."

*"Who gave Himself for us, that He
might redeem us from all iniquity,
and purify unto Himself a peculiar
people, zealous of good works."*

Titus 2:14

REFLECTION PAGE

WHAT IS YOUR FIRST REACTION AFTER LISTENING/READING THIS SONG?

DID THIS SONG INSPIRE YOU TO INCREASE YOUR RELATIONSHIP WITH GOD? WHY?

HOW MUCH DOES MUSIC MINISTRY FIT INTO YOUR WORSHIP?

CHAPTER 50

"THE LORD'S PRAYER"

Written by: Jesus Christ

"The Lord's Prayer," is the heart and center of Christianity. Taught to us by Jesus Christ, the prayer is not necessarily the only prayer one can offer to God, but it is the most specifically and well-designed for honoring and recognizing God as the One who always has been and always will be: the Great I Am!

"The Lord's Prayer," also called, *Our Father* or *Pater Noster,* is a central Christian prayer which Jesus taught as the way to pray. Two versions of this prayer are recorded in the gospels: a longer form within the *Sermon on the Mount* in the *Gospel of Matthew,* and a shorter form in the *Gospel of Luke.*

Some have suggested that both were original, the Matthean version spoken by Jesus early in His ministry in Galilee, and Lucan version one year later, possibly in Judea.

"...Thy kingdom come, Thy will be done on earth as it is in heaven..." tells us God's will is as dominant and powerful in Heaven as here on earth.

"...lead us not into temptation, but deliver us from evil..." we are asking His help in avoiding trouble and keeping us safe from all that would harm us.

"...forgive us our debts as we forgive our debtors..." we are asking His forgiveness and acknowledging we will forgive those who have hurt or sinned against us.

MICHAEL E. PAYTON, MA

"Our Father, which art
In heaven, hollowed be
Thy name"

"Thy kingdom come,
Thy will be done on
Earth as it is in heaven"

"Give us this day our daily bread
And forgive us our debts
As we forgive our debtors"

"And lead us not into temptation
But deliver us from evil"

"For Thine is the kingdom
And the power
And the glory forever,
Amen"

"For Thine is the kingdom
And the power
And the glory forever,
Amen"

REFLECTION PAGE

WHAT IS YOUR FIRST REACTION AFTER LISTENING/READING THIS SONG?

DID THIS SONG INSPIRE YOU TO INCREASE YOUR RELATIONSHIP WITH GOD? WHY?

HOW MUCH DOES MUSIC MINISTRY FIT INTO YOUR WORSHIP?

ACKNOWLEDGEMENTS

MY SPECIAL THANKS TO THE FOLLOWING
FOR ASSISTING IN THE
RESEARCH AND SELECTION OF SONGS

Vicki Payton
Sharon Lute
Callie Kurtz
Olivia Kurtz

Printed in the United States
by Baker & Taylor Publisher Services